NO GREATER SACRIFICE, NO GREATER LOVE

*A Son's Journey
to Normandy*

NO GREATER SACRIFICE, NO GREATER LOVE

WALTER FORD CARTER

with TERRY GOLWAY

Smithsonian Books • Washington

Copy editor: Gretchen Smith Mui
Production editor: Joanne Reams
Designer: Janice Wheeler

Library of Congress Cataloging-in-Publication data

Carter, Walter Ford, 1940–
No greater sacrifice, no greater love : a son's journey to Normandy /
Walter Ford Carter with Terry Golway
p.   cm.
ISBN 1-58834-159-3 (alk. paper)
1. Carter, Elmer Norval, 1977–1944. 2. Carter, Emma Ferne, 1912–1995.
3. United States. Army—Medical personnel—Biography. 4. Army
spouses—United States—Biography. 5. World War, 1939–1945—
Campaigns—France—Normandy. I. Title.

D811.A2C355   2004
940.4'1442'0922—dc22

2003070384

British Library Cataloging-in-Publication Data are available
Manufactured in the United States of America
09 08 07 06 05 04   1 2 3 4 5

∞The paper used in this publication meets the minimum requirements of
the American Standard for Information Sciences—Permanence of Paper
for Printed Library materials ANSI Z39.48- 1992.

Frontispiece caption: Norval, Fernie, and their

young family, September 1940.

To my parents

Contents

Discovery

1   There was no mystery about it. Nobody held out false hopes. There was no talk of a miracle. My mother was dying, and she knew it. It was May 1995, and she was lying in a hospital bed at home, recovering from surgery to remove a tumor from her pancreas and intestine. The surgery had failed, and there was nothing more the doctors could do.

    I had taken her home to the house she had shared ever so briefly with my father before he went off to war, in the town—Huntington, West Virginia—where she had been born, where she and my father had met as children, where she had reared their two sons, and where she had found some measure of comfort as she grew old.

I tried to prepare myself for her final moments, thinking about what I would say to her, what she might say to me. I hoped that we might even talk about a subject we had never truly discussed: my father.

In just a few days, thousands of old soldiers would commemorate the fifty-first anniversary of D-Day, and the media would duly note the sacrifice offered that day in the name of freedom. My mother would not live to see the anniversary, but it may not have mattered anyway. She paid little attention to these ceremonies. They would have reminded her of a more painful, more personal occasion—the day she learned that she was a war widow.

Dr. Elmer Norval Carter, a captain and battalion surgeon with the 115th Regiment of the Twenty-ninth Infantry Division, landed on Omaha Beach in the late morning of June 6, 1944. He had volunteered for the US Army in 1942, when I was two years old and my brother, Tom, was five. Fathers were exempt from the draft at the time, but my father, who was serving as examining physician for the local draft board, believed his place was in the service. His country needed him.

After basic training, he sailed across the Atlantic in late 1942 and was appointed chief of psychiatry at an army hospital in southern England, even though he had little experience in the field. In the army's eyes, however, my father's brief tenure as a staff physician in a West Virginia psychiatric hospital made him a psychiatrist. If nothing else, it was a safe job, far from the front lines. But my father wanted to play a more active role, and in March 1944 he obtained a transfer to the Twenty-ninth Infantry Division, which was training for D-Day. On that

A newly enlisted Norval Carter, first lieutenant, in his US Army uniform, July 1942. This is the photograph that Fernie kept on her bedroom bureau.

day he was aboard a landing craft in the English Channel, part of the largest amphibious assault in history. He survived the carnage on Omaha Beach, but eleven days later, on June 17, as the Allies were pushing inland into France, a German sniper killed him as he tended to a wounded soldier near an orchard outside St.-Lô.

The telegram that arrived on July 6 informed my mother that the love of her life, the big, strapping man who called her Fernie, was dead. The extended family, alerted to the bad news, rushed to our house, where they found my mother collapsed in a chair. My cousin, Jennie Anne, took me outside for a walk. I chatted with her, telling her that I would soon have a baby sister, once Daddy came home from the war.

I was four years old, Tom seven. My mother was thirty-two.

I grew up knowing my father as a smiling face behind glass. My mother kept a photograph of him on her bedroom bureau. He looked so young and dashing: Captain E. Norval Carter, forever thirty-two years old.

I treasured several other images of him, not from photographs but from my memories. I see him standing on the deck of a paddle wheeler on the Ohio River, about a mile and a half from our home in Huntington. He has just taken my brother and me on a boat ride. The sight of the powerful paddle wheel churning up the water frightens me, but I do not cry because my father is nearby. I see him standing shirtless in his shorts, hands on hips, at the end of our second-floor hallway. He is smiling. I am just out of the bath and in my pajamas, standing at the other end of the hall, waiting for my goodnight hug. And I see him as he walks through our front door. He has been away at basic training but has been given leave to return home for the weekend. My mother, my brother, and I are eating lunch in the kitchen, but when we hear him we jump up and charge into the living room. And there he is. He and my mother embrace, as Tom and I run about and shout.

My mother never remarried, never dated again. In photographs of her from that time, she looks too thin, and her smile is wan at best. Throughout America during the 1940s, tens of thousands of women received telegrams informing them of the death of their husbands and expressing the condolences of a grateful nation. In some ways, these women were and remain uncelebrated heroes of that celebrated age. Grief stricken, most of them courageously went on as best they could, if only for the sake of their children. My mother was one of these heroic women. I saw her cry only a few times. The first was in the summer of 1944, when I was four years old, not long after that dreaded telegram arrived. Impatient to go outside to play with a friend, I went into the kitchen and found her sobbing, her face contorted with grief. She lifted her head from her arms, folded on the table in front of her. "What is it?" she asked. Stunned, I blurted out my request, and when she said yes, I beat a hasty retreat.

Although there were doubtless other such moments of pure grief, I remember none as vividly. I do remember that there was rarely any conversation about my father or the war. For more than a year my mother could not bring herself even to mention his name.

More than ever, my brother and I became the center of my mother's world. Beyond our home life, she worked in a series of community service administrative jobs, played the violin in the local symphony, and took refuge in painting, reading, playing bridge, and socializing with three or four close friends.

As the years went on, she helped rear my brother's oldest child when he married and became a father while still in his teens. Her burdens increased as she grew older, for it fell to her to care for aging relatives. She never complained, although she sometimes seemed weary. In the end, she reflected that she had derived satisfaction from her life of service to her family.

All the while, over the decades of her life, she rarely spoke about my father. And now, as she approached her own death, the silence on the subject remained intact. We talked instead about other family members or what we were watching on television. We listened to music together. Or we were silent. I was afraid to speak about my father or about my brother, Tom, who had died in a plane crash in 1972, leaving behind three sons, for fear that she would be overcome by the grief she had repressed for so many years.

We should have talked about Dad years ago, I thought, but now was not the time to begin that conversation.

On the morning of May 27, in my mother's living room, I was playing some of the music we loved— several slow movements from Bach's Suites for Cello, which I played on the trombone, and recordings of Schubert's String Quintet in C, Ewald's Brass Quintet no. 1, and the Modern Jazz Quartet's "Django."

Jennie Anne, now a nurse, had been caring for my mother. Just before ten o'clock, she came in and told me that my mother was about to die. It was time to say goodbye.

I sat close to my mother and told her that I loved her. She was staring at the ceiling. I then voiced some of what had been on my mind for so long: "Ever since I was a small boy, I've had a mental picture of Dad, smiling with an expression of love, watching me. Then, after Tom died, I have often seen the two of them together, smiling, watching me. Now I know that I'll see the three of you together, smiling, watching me. And one day down the road I will join you. Then we will be together again, happy."

Her eyes suddenly focused. Her chest rose with a slower, heavier breath. One tear crept down her face, but she was beyond reply. Two hours later she died.

After the rituals of farewell and burial, my mother's family and some friends gathered in her house to share memories. My brother's sons, grown men now, had come to Huntington from their homes in Alaska. It was a sunny day, and we sat on the porch while several women from my mother's church served sandwiches. We listened closely as two of my parents' friends reminisced about the 1930s, when they were young doctors just starting out. Inevitably, they spoke about the war and how all of their friends had come home alive—except for my father. One of them mentioned the last letter he had received from my father, in May 1944, while he was in England awaiting, like thousands of Allied soldiers, the order to board transports for the hundred-mile trip across the English Channel. In his letter, my father confessed a secret he had withheld from my mother: He had volunteered for combat duty with the Twenty-ninth Division. I knew that he had volunteered for the army, but I did not know that he had actually requested a high-risk assignment, had chosen to join a division training for the invasion of France. What was more, my father had written that he would never tell Fernie what he had done. Although it depressed him, he wrote, to think that he might never see his wife and sons again, he did not fear death.

My children, Norman and Catherine, and my three nephews were transfixed by this story of the grandfather they had never known. Sandwiches, drinks, and even other guests were ignored as my parents' friends told stories we had never heard before. Catherine, looking at all the people whom my father had never met and who never had a chance to know him, said angrily to herself, "How could he do such a thing? How could he have placed himself in danger when he had so much to live for?"

It was a question I too had asked when contemplating the fact that he had volunteered for the service in the first place, even though he was exempt from the draft, even though he had two small sons and a young wife. How could he have done such a thing?

After my mother's funeral my wife, Bonnie, and I stayed in Huntington for several days to take care

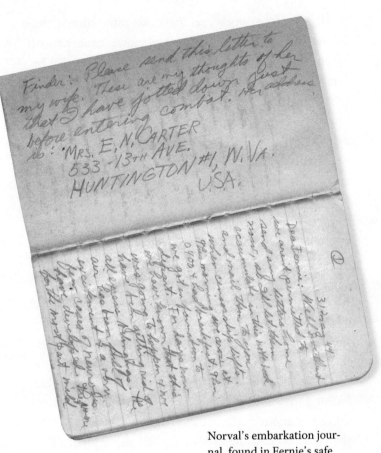

Norval's embarkation journal, found in Fernie's safe deposit box after her death.

of all the paperwork and housekeeping chores that accompany death. My mother had rented a safe deposit box in a local bank, so that too was on our to-do list before we returned to our home and our lives in Newton, Massachusetts. The old Guaranty Bank was in a relatively new, two-story red brick building just over a mile from my mother's home. Her affairs were in relatively good order, and she had put the deposit box in both our names many years earlier.

The deposit box was tucked in a drawer in a back room that had to be opened by an attendant. In it I found a small, pocket-sized notebook, fairly old. On the inside cover were a few handwritten lines: "Finder: Please send this letter to my wife. These are my thoughts of her that I have jotted down just before entering combat. Her address is: Mrs. E. N. Carter, 533-13th Avenue, Huntington, West Virginia." The handwriting was my father's. Here in my hands was a record of his last days on earth.

I remembered seeing the notebook years ago when I joined my mother on an errand to the bank. When I asked her about it, she brushed aside my question. "Oh, that's just something of your Dad's," she said, in a tone that implied I should not pursue the subject. I took the hint and thought no more about the mysteries its pages might contain. Seeing the notebook, all these years later, I could hardly contain my curiosity. I quickly collected everything in the box and returned home.

As curious as I was, I could not bring myself to read the notebook right away. I needed to steel myself before embarking on what I knew would be an emotional journey into the past. The following morning I rose early and went out to sit on my mother's porch. I opened the notebook and began to read. Inside were entries dated from May 31 to June 4, 1944. In the days leading up to D-Day, my father and the 150,000 other soldiers destined for Normandy were not allowed to write home, so my father had written in the notebook instead:

May 31, 1944

Dear Fernie:

Well, sweetheart, we aren't permitted to send any letters home now, so I'll let them accumulate in this notebook and mail them to you when censorship lifts.

This morning we rose at 0400 and had breakfast. Then we got in formation to depart. For days now we have known that this was going to happen and we have been getting rid of all excess belongings. The air has been full of excitement and a very few cases of neurosis have developed. They were for the most part mild panic states and were easily controlled. . . .

Our particular battalion has been briefed and the mission has been studied in detail. We don't make the initial breakthrough on our sector but we follow in about 4 hours to secure the ground and clean up any resistance. We must get 10 miles inland on the first day. This may be tough or it may be easy.

The entry for June 1 read:

I awoke at 0500 hrs, Fernie, and lay there thinking of you, wondering if we shall ever see each other again. While lying there many things came to mind; how I used to hold you in my arms and tell you I loved you. Nothing must happen to prevent our being together. . . .

Why is it that I am not afraid? It is normal to be

afraid under the circumstances but yet I just am not afraid. Perhaps I shall be when we hit the far shore. I do feel a detached sort of concern as to whether I shall see you and the boys again, and I have that dull ache of longing to be back home with you all, but the constriction and tremulousness and the instability of fear—well, I don't have it. Maybe it would be best if I were a bit fearful.

On June 4, as my father prepared to sail across the English Channel, he wrote:

Fernie, my sweetheart, I feel I shall see you again. You and the boys. But if I don't, I want you all to remember that my love for you cannot be said or put on paper. It can only be felt. You have meant everything to me that is good and happy. Since tomorrow is D-Day (and we weigh anchor tonight), I won't be able to write for a few days. May God help us in our mission. I hope to return to you all. God bless you Fernie, you Tom, and you Walter Ford.

Until this moment, my knowledge of my father had been based on a few anecdotes told by family and friends. Now for the first time I was hearing him speak directly. He called me by my full name, Walter Ford.

There was more.

Along with the notebook was a letter from my father dated May 4, 1944. It was addressed to Tom and me:

It has been a long time since we have written to one another but your mother has told me some mighty nice things about you both. It seems that you are doing all those things that boys do: grow, lose teeth, get sick, go to school, learn new tricks, and pay homage to some girl. My, but it would be fun to be home and watch you do these things! I would like to joke with you & talk things over, sort of man to man, you know. Fernie seems to be very proud of you both, and it is no wonder that she is. You must send me the pictures that are being taken so I can sort of imagine myself talking to you now & then.

In several more months, perhaps, this war will be over and then we can really enjoy doing things together. Then we can go for hikes, or go on the river and really have some fine talks. Sitting and talking is the best pastime there is, Tom, and I believe you will enjoy it more than W.F. But Walter Ford, you will like it somewhat too, and we shall get our heads together & figure out something that you will like. . . .

I want you always to be happy. Always try to do things the good way & it will give you peace of mind & happiness. You won't always be able to do things the "good way." You will do things wrong at times, all persons do. But if you are sorry for doing things wrong, the chances are you will do much better on future occasions. When you make a mistake (and you will make plenty of them!), don't become too tearful or blue. . . . Keep your sense of humor about you. Always be able to laugh at yourself and with other people.

Take good care of your mother and also take good care of the advice & help she has to offer you. It may seem at times that she has more of the former than the latter, but the opposite is true. She can really help you. She can make you happy when you are sad. She can lighten your worries. She can make things seem sensible where there is apparently no sense. . . .

Tom, I was giving a lecture to a group of officers and non-coms night before last, on the treatment of mental & emotional troubles due to an upheaval of the spirit. One usually thinks this kind of treatment is carried out mostly by medical specialists (called psychiatrists). But such is not the case. I pointed out to them that the giving of sympathetic advice & help is a treatment that is dispensed more by mothers than by any other group. So remember in the future that your mother can help you with a lot of troubles. You are fortunate also in having a mother who is very wise, very sweet, and who will lean over backwards to help you out.

My father's concern for us, now expressed so directly, was a revelation. I wanted to share my discovery with my children and my brother's children, who knew almost nothing about this man who smiled out at them from picture frames in their grandmother's house.

Several days earlier Catherine had found a box of letters in my mother's attic. Many were arranged in bundles and tied with a yellow ribbon. I had seen the collection once before, in my late teens, when I was cleaning up the sunroom one day. I read two or three of them, put them back, and told my mother what I had done. She looked hurt. "Don't I have any privacy for things of my own?" Later, when I returned to the sunroom, the letters had vanished, and I never again raised the subject. I thought about them during her final illness but decided not to ask about them. In fact, I thought the letters might no longer exist.

But they did—dozens and dozens of them. Catherine had discovered the missing story of my father's life, the story my mother could not bring herself to tell me. Now that she was beyond suffering, however, she would allow me to discover my father, in his own words, through the letters she had so carefully preserved.

The letters went as far back as the early 1920s, before my parents were teenagers. There were love letters from school days, letters filled with barely disguised adolescent yearnings, letters that captured a time and a place lost to history—a small town in West Virginia, before superhighways, before the age of mass consumption.

I could not read them all right away. We were too busy sorting out my mother's possessions. I brought them home to Newton, and over the course of many months I came to know the smiling man in the photographs. I found my father.

After I had read every line, after I had absorbed what this man was teaching me a half century after his death, I had an answer to my daughter's question: "How could he have done such a thing?"

He did it because of who he was: Dr. Elmer Norval Carter, captain in the US Army.

Walter Ford celebrating his first birthday with his father and brother, May 13, 1941.

2

I was born into a world at war, on May 13, 1940, the very day Winston Churchill addressed the British House of Commons for the first time as prime minister. Speaking to his worried colleagues and a fearful nation, he acknowledged that he had nothing to offer "but blood, toil, tears and sweat."

Three days earlier, Hitler's army and air force had smashed through Belgium, the Netherlands, and Luxembourg—neutral nations all—on their way to France. The lightning assault marked the end of nearly eight months of military paralysis in Europe following Hitler's invasion of Poland the preceding September.

Europe was in flames, while imperial Japan was on the march in Asia.

In the United States, Franklin Delano Roosevelt would soon launch his campaign for an unprecedented third term, promising that "we will not participate in foreign wars . . . except in case of attack." The fighting—in China, in western Europe, in Africa—was thousands of miles away, and the United States remained untouched.

Still, the war cast a long and fearsome shadow. I can only imagine the anxiety with which my parents followed the news from Europe and Asia. Radio brought Edward R. Murrow's descriptions of the Battle of Britain into American living rooms. They heard the hysterical voice of Hitler, ranting before cheering Nazis; the growl of Churchill, spitting defiance at the German dictator; and the confident, patrician tones of Roosevelt.

In 1940 my parents were just getting established after several years of wandering Depression-era America in search of better jobs and brighter futures. Earlier in the year, with my brother in tow, they had returned to their hometown, Huntington, West Virginia, where my father went into private medical practice with a friend.

War was not part of the dream my parents shared for each other and for their children, but now there was no escaping events beyond their control. The capitals of Europe were under attack, the menace of dictatorship threatened millions, and every day in some faraway battlefield soldiers and civilians alike died by the hundreds and thousands.

War had not yet come to America. And yet war was everywhere.

Before I was a year old, my father received a letter dated April 21, 1941, from the governor of West Virginia, informing him that the president of the United States had appointed him an examining physician with the local draft board. President Roosevelt, after winning his third term, had ordered a peacetime draft and mobilized the National Guard to bolster the country's small and poorly equipped armed services.

On December 7, 1941, the nation's worst fears were realized when the Japanese attacked Pearl Harbor. Three days later, Germany and Italy declared war on the United States. The war was no longer something that Americans simply heard about in the news. It was at our doorstep.

During the ensuing months, as America geared up for global conflict, my father decided that his place was with the young men who were trading civilian clothes for military uniforms. I do not know whether he discussed this decision with his own father, a Spanish-American War veteran. I do not know what conversations he might have had with my mother.

I do know that although the government was draft-

Tom playing doctor with his little brother, Christmas 1940.

ing hundreds of thousands of civilians, my father was exempt because he had two young children. (Fathers did not become eligible for the draft until 1943.) Still, many young men volunteered rather than wait for a draft notice, because enlisting allowed them to choose their branch of service.

In May 1942 my parents bought a house on the south side of town, no more than a mile from the homes in which each had grown up. The deed was recorded in my mother's name only—by then my father had made his decision to enlist.

It was during these months of preparation for war that I formed some of the few memories I have of my father. I remember him as a well-built man with broad shoulders and an erect bearing. The image is confirmed by his army records, which state that he was 6 feet tall and weighed 185 pounds. His feet were long but narrow, AAA width. A handsome man with a genuine smile, he was an engaged citizen of his hometown. His patients loved him, as did the children and board members of the town's Children's Clinic, where he volunteered to provide health care for the poor. His colleagues had invited him to join the Junior Medical Society.

On July 7, 1942, as millions of young men throughout America trained for battle against hardened professional soldiers in Europe and Asia, Dr. E. Norval Carter was appointed a first lieutenant in the Army Medical Corps. The life he had known and wished to share with his wife and children meant everything to him, but he believed that his place was with those who would fight—and die—to defend his country's liberty.

The Children's Clinic board adopted a resolution thanking him for his work with the poor, and the board's chairman wished him "the best of luck in your new field of endeavor."

That new field was to be the battlefield.

My father was born in Huntington, West Virginia, on October 17, 1911, the only child of Eustace and Sapho Carter. Eustace had little formal education but no shortage of determination and independence—one day after an argument with his teacher he quit school in a huff. Eustace and his family lived in the rural town of Milton, about 10 miles east of Huntington. His father, Salem Carter, ran a carriage and livery service and was deputy sheriff.

When America went to war with Spain in 1898, Eustace enlisted in the army and served in the Philippines. In truth, it was not much of a war—it was over quickly and ended in an overwhelming victory for the United States. My grandfather rarely spoke about his service, so as a child my father heard no romantic tales about the glory of war.

Eustace Carter married Sapho Bryan, the daughter of a doctor who practiced medicine in Huntington, the town Eustace and Sapho chose to make their home. Huntington owed its existence to one of the marvels of post–Civil War America: the railroads. Located on the southern edge of the Ohio River where Ohio, Kentucky, and West Virginia meet, Huntington was incorporated in 1871 to serve as a terminal for the Chesapeake & Ohio Railroad, which linked the cities and towns of the eastern seaboard to the

Ohio River and the Midwest. The C&O's tracks divided the town, with the downtown business district on the north side and the tree-lined residential neighborhoods on the south. With its convenient access to rail and river, Huntington quickly grew to become a thriving, small industrial city.

Eustace Carter was among the many Huntington residents who went to work for the C&O. He eventually rose to become a freight-train conductor, a good, solid job that he held onto after the stock market crash of 1929. The C&O transported coal to factories and utilities, and even during the Great Depression those plants needed the C&O's services. This steady demand protected my grandfather from unemployment and allowed him to send his son to college and medical school, although the work often kept him away from home.

Eustace and Sapho gave their son an uncommon combination of names. Where his unusual middle name, Norval, came from is uncertain, but he preferred it to his first name, Elmer, which he associated with backwater, rural America, although sometimes he enjoyed posing as a hayseed. Eustace and Sapho had their hands full with this spirited, red-haired little boy. When he was unruly or otherwise disobedient, Sapho smothered him in a bear hug on her lap until he quieted down or repented.

In 1922, when Norval was eleven, the Carter family built a substantial two-story red-brick house diagonally across the street from the Lowry family. Three years earlier the Lowrys had suffered a terrible loss when Thomas Lowry, a lawyer, died of a stroke at the age of fifty-seven. He left behind his widow, Anna, and four children. Three were already young adults, but the youngest was only seven years old. Her name was Emma Ferne.

She was born on March 6, 1912, something of a late-in-life surprise for Thomas and Anna. Without siblings near her own age, Emma Ferne had to look outside the home for playmates. As luck would have it, when she was ten years old, a boy who had no brothers or sisters to play with moved into the new house across the street. My parents met and became fast friends.

When they entered Cammack Junior High, they rode their bicycles to and from school every day, and before long the two adolescents began to think of themselves as more than just neighbors and friends. In junior high school, Norval sent a note to Fernie, whom he addressed as "Dear, dearest, more dear": "Let's get up at 7:00 and I will come over at your house or you will come here," he wrote, closing with "Love, love, all my love." Underneath his signature, in the time-honored fashion of love-struck teens, he drew a heart with an arrow through it and with their initials: ENC + EFL.

Norval and Fernie during their junior high school years, 1926.

Norval's youth was idyllic. He had lots of friends, some of whom he would remain close to for the rest of his life, and they were always welcome in his home, often gathering on his front porch. His sweetheart lived a few steps away, and they started their days together not long after sunrise. The West Virginia summers were filled with long days at play, visits to downtown Huntington, bicycle rides, and hikes. Fernie and Norval were constant companions, and they grew even closer during their years at Huntington High School.

Eventually this fledgling romance required a certain formality, and one evening Mrs. Lowry invited Norval to dinner with the family. He left an indelible first impression, although perhaps not the kind he intended. At one point during the meal, he used the tablecloth to wipe his silverware. The Lowrys were astonished at this display of barbarism. Noticing their surprise, he commented simply, "That's how we do it at our house."

The summer of 1927, just after ninth grade, separated the young pair. Fernie left Huntington for two trips, the first to attend Camp Fire Girls camp in Barboursville, just east of Huntington, and then, in late August, to visit her friend Mary Cloe, who had recently moved to Charleston, nearly 50 miles away. Although they were not apart for long, it was long enough to inspire sentimental thoughts, as fifteen-year-old Fernie confessed: "You know about the old saying, 'Absence makes the heart grow fonder'? Well, it sure is right. I wish you were here tonight. … I guess you think me silly but I get that way sometimes."

During her visit to Charleston, Fernie wrote another

letter revealing that teenage girls during the Jazz Age were as body conscious as they are today. She was about 5 feet, 4 inches tall, with very dark brown, almost black, hair, which she parted on one side, sweeping the bangs dramatically to the other side. In none of the photographs from that time does she seem the slightest bit overweight, but she reported that she was dieting and had lost four pounds. She was coming of age at a time when the glamorous flappers of the Roaring Twenties, with their slender waistlines and thin arms, were very much in vogue.

The following summer Fernie and Norval endured a longer separation when he, a clarinet player, joined the local Boy Scout band for a tour of West Virginia and Ohio. Before he left, the young sweethearts had a serious talk about the future. That much is clear from a letter that Mary Cloe wrote to Norval in June 1928, when he was a few months shy of seventeen and Fernie was barely sixteen: "Since I know your wonderful secret, Fernie has seemed closer to me than ever. . . . She'll make a wonderful wife—that's all I can say—for what more could I say?"

The letter suggests that Fernie and Norval had talked about getting married in 1930, the year they would graduate from high school. Although that was two years away, Mary and Fernie went window-shopping for rings in downtown Charleston. "We seem so young for such things," Mary wrote to Norval, sketching a romantic picture:

> I can just see you sitting on the front porch of a little white cottage smoking or reading the paper. In a little

while Fernie comes out. She has been fixing up after supper. She has on pale green, her hair in waves and down low on her neck. Can't you just see her as she stands there in the fading light of dusk? Immediately you put down your paper and you have a comfortable radiantly happy evening together. Won't it be wonderful? The nearest heaven that's possible on this earth.

Norval had already decided that he would become a doctor; Fernie had her own dreams of attending Wellesley College in Massachusetts, which seemed to her the epitome of elegance, refinement, and the good life. How did they plan to achieve these lofty goals as teenage newlyweds? Only young lovers would know.

Although Fernie's letters to Norval during the summer of 1928 are filled with schoolgirl frivolity, she was a serious, gifted student. She was a member of the Scribbler's Club, an "honor literary society" whose goal was to "foster an appreciation of literature through the development of individual talent." She joined the Girl Reserves, which encouraged members to "face life squarely" and organized toy drives and Thanksgiving baskets, among other community-minded deeds. She also played the violin in the school orchestra.

Fernie finished her second year in high school with grades that did nothing to discourage her college dream—most of her final marks were high. She was hardly satisfied, however, describing the 90 she received in biology as "not so good." But she took comfort in noting that her 93 in geometry was considerably higher than Norval's 80. He was often the despair of his teachers, who thought he did not try hard enough.

As the summer of 1928—and their separation—neared its conclusion, Norval wrote to Fernie from the countryside near Akron, Ohio, where the night before some of his friends had "some wild experiences." He was discreet enough not to spell out what these big-city experiences had been, but he did tell Fernie how much he missed her: "Gee, I sure wish you were where I am now. Out in the 'sticks' sitting by a brook—everything is almost complete. Dear heart, how I would like to have just one kiss from you. It would be like a new life, or something great from paradise."

For Fernie and Norval, 1930—their senior year in high school—was an eventful year. Fittingly, their pictures in the yearbook were adjacent. The editors wrote of Norval: "His cheerful grin and clever remarks make him a favorite." Of Fernie they noted that she had "a subtle sense of humor and a certain come-hither expression in her eyes." In his copy of the yearbook, Norval printed "WANTED!" across the top of Fernie's picture and her telephone number across the bottom.

But the wretched economy meant that there would be no wedding for them that year. For Fernie a second dream died as well; she would not be attending Wellesley—her family simply could not afford it. Her widowed mother had limited funds, and the nation was in the grip of the Great Depression. Instead, she en-rolled in Marshall College, right there in town, and so did Norval.

By early June he was on his way to Texas to visit a friend who had moved away from Huntington two years earlier. As he had during his band trip in 1928, he kept a journal of his travels. It is a record of a vanished time and place: the Bible Belt South during the Hoover administration, before rural electrification and before the repeal of Prohibition, before the freeway and the strip mall, and long before integration.

June 7. Woke up and got up at 6:00 (at the Y in Louisville). There are many beautiful girls here. They have keen forms too. I went over to the public library and read some. This building is very pretty & has over twice as many books as our library does. Maxine, one of the

Norval's and Fernie's senior photographs in their high school yearbook, 1930.

ELMER CARTER
"Hearts yearn for all they earn."
Hi-Y, Airplane, Physics, Orchestra.
His cheerful grin and clever remarks make him a favorite.

Deceased
Doctor Married Emferne Lowry

MADOLYN TROWBRIDGE
"Smile and the men smile at you."
Torch, Scribblers, Art, Dramatic, Commercial, Sec. Dramatic '29-'30, Sec. Commercial '30, Sec. Torch '30, Sec. of Service '30.
Madolyn is artistically inclined—she likes to study art. She is a study for an artist herself.

Deceased

EMFERNE LOWRY
"Begone dull care, thou and I shall never agree."
Scribblers, Crucible, Girl Reserves, Latin, Art, College, Orchestra '28-'29-'30, Art, Fiddlin' a subtle sense of humor, and a certain come hither expression in her eyes are Em's long suits—step up and take a bow Em.

BILL JOHNSON
"None but the brave deserve the fair."
Hi-Y '28-'29, Orchestra '28-'29.
Bill is a collector of antiques—witness the "chevy."

librarians (I didn't get her last name) invited me over to her "living quarters." I didn't know exactly what she meant, but I do know that we would have had one swell time if I could have stayed in town. Cruel woild!

You know when a fellow is used to being exposed to just a few girls and then is by himself in a large city that is full of "beauties" he feels sort of —well—I can't explain it.

The small-town boy who suddenly found himself in big cities for the first time was disconcerted. He had fallen in love with the girl across the street, but now, in places like Louisville, he was meeting women the likes of whom he had never seen. During a short stay at the Hotel Avon in Biloxi, Mississippi, he took a walk along a beach, listened to some "soft, seducing" jazz, and couldn't help but notice the "beautiful, wild women." The following day, after watching some of the locals catch shrimp—and getting a sunburn in the process—he met a woman at his hotel who was, in Norval's words, "out for a good time." They had a few drinks together. "She proved to be very entertaining and a jolly good sport. She wanted me to stay over awhile, but I thought it best not to on account of— Well, I want to see New Orleans."

Fernie and Norval started at Marshall College together in 1930, but my father—a restless soul, always in search of adventure—transferred to West Virginia University in Morgantown for his sophomore year and then to the University of Alabama for his junior year. His course load was heavy—during his first semester at WVU, he spent thirty-eight hours per week in the classroom, taking quantitative chemistry, physi-

Fernie with her favorite of the many musical instruments she played. After hearing some chamber music in Liverpool, England, Norval wrote to his sons: "It . . . made me think of your mother and how she plays" (August 10, 1943).

cal chemistry, zoology, physics, German, and military science. He also ran track, swam, played intramural baseball, and got beaten up in the boxing ring. "I . . . am damned near punch drunk!" he wrote to Fernie after one particularly tough session.

Meanwhile, at Marshall College Fernie double-majored in English and music education. She also taught music to local seventh and eighth graders, and, as if that were not enough, for a few weeks she filled in for one of the college's music instructors, teaching clarinet, trumpet, cello, violin, and trombone. "Don't ever teach school, sweetheart," she complained to Norval, "because it is the hardest work I ever got into."

As he moved from college to college and from place to place, Norval became more serious about his future and his life with Fernie. While at the University of Alabama, he wrote:

> Sweetheart, I am so homesick for you that I just feel like I haven't got a friend in the world. It may sound child-like, but dearest, I—oh, hell! I can't describe how I feel. I can't work or do anything it seems. . . . God! If we could only get married and go on to school together. Do you feel like this? I surely do pity you if you do.
>
> For the first time in my life I realize that I need you. I really want to lay my head in your lap and let you run your fingers through my hair and oh—dammit, don't laugh but I guess I am one love-sick fool.

Norval was undecided whether he should attend medical school in Virginia beginning in the fall of 1933 or remain in Alabama. He was interested in performing experiments in embryology and zoology, but continuing to do research "would prolong the time before our marriage." By January 1933 he had waited long enough.

> Somehow, regardless of how, we must plan to be married and maybe be together before I finish medicine. It's not just selfishness on my part, but it is the fact that I really need you. I know that I could do better and more efficient work if things were like that. I realize that I have my moments of laziness (and they always come at the wrong time!), but if you were with me it would steady me a lot and make a different man of me, don't you think so?

In the winter of 1933, Norval decided to apply to the Medical College of Virginia in Richmond without finishing his bachelor's degree at the University of Alabama. One of Huntington's most distinguished citizens, Dr. Walter Vest—for whom I am named—was an alumnus of MCV and had mentored many of the town's aspiring doctors. Dr. Vest, who proudly wore his Phi Beta Kappa key on the vest of his three-piece suit, was the Carter family's physician and friend. Naturally, Norval consulted him before applying. In a letter dated March 30, the medical school congratulated him on his acceptance.

With medical school on the horizon, Norval's thoughts continued to focus on Fernie and their future. "I am sort of tired being a bachelor for the past thousand years," he told her. "It is just about time to try marriage." That was easier said than done. During the summer, after he returned home from Alabama, Fernie, who had finished her college degree in three years, was hired as a teacher at a high school in the coal-mining town of Colcord, West Virginia, about 90 miles from Huntington. Her new job—her first—would begin in the fall, the same time that Norval was scheduled to start medical school in Richmond.

On September 6, 1933—a few months after Adolf Hitler became chancellor of Germany and just days before my father was to begin medical school—Fernie and Norval and three friends piled into a car and drove 12 miles into Kentucky, to the town of Catlettsburg. There, by the authority of a local clergyman and with their friends as the only guests, my parents were married. Their families were surprised by the means but not the result. In later years my mother would say they eloped because they did not have enough money for a traditional wedding; certainly the Lowrys were in no position to pay for one. My father, however, had a different view. In a nostalgic letter written while he was in the army, he recalled, "I remember the summer of our marriage, how I lost patience and cussed you out & said we would be married the next day or else! And we were married."

They began their lives together by living apart. After a few days as husband and wife in Huntington, Fernie went on to Colcord to begin teaching, and Norval journeyed to Richmond to start medical school. A short time after Fernie left home, she received a letter from her sister, Becky: "We were all talking about your acquiring an A.B. degree, a husband, and a school in one month," she wrote. "What a woman, what a woman!" My mother paid a quick visit to Huntington and took care of some postwedding chores, such as having her rings engraved with their initials. "I also ordered announcements & picked out the silver," she told her husband. "I selected 'Normandie' pattern. I hope you'll like it."

The joy of marriage quickly gave way to old routines—writing long letters to each other as a substitute for being together. For the moment, they had no other choice.

Fernie did not adjust well to the rural experience, especially rooming with six other teachers in the countryside. She told my father that she would lie awake at night, unable to sleep as she listened to "the cow bells tinkle, pigs grunt, rooster crow & even a panther screamed down the road—at least they all said it was a panther." She and the other teachers walked 2 miles from their residence to the school, where she was in charge of students who were, as she described them, "twice as large" as she was.

Norval, in the meantime, seemed intent on living up to his reputation as a practical joker. He became known on campus for such stunts as eating chalk or even a frog's leg if all of his classmates paid him a dime. (This was the Depression, after all.) The most famous of these episodes, one that many of his classmates would remember for decades, involved a jar of sour pickles. To earn his dimes, he ate every last pickle. Then he raced to the bathroom, where the pickles reappeared. A few years later one of his friends wrote in his yearbook, "Loved the pickles!"

My father's humor and good nature served him well when he was chosen, along with several other students, to spend a school year at City Home, a charity

Norval, in the middle with pipe, arm sling, and head bandage, hamming it up with classmates at the Medical College of Virginia, 1935.

hospital run by the city of Richmond for indigent, chronically ill patients. Although the aspiring doctors were treating very ill people and were on call twenty-four hours a day, Norval found ways to make people laugh. One of his fellow students remembered that he was "always full of fun . . . always doing practical jokes and annoying the professors. But everybody loved him because he was such a friendly, wonderful person with no malice or bad thoughts about anyone."

The professors at the Medical College of Virginia, however, did not always see the humor of Norval's antics, and perhaps with good reason. He kept a pistol by his bed, and he developed a habit of firing it into the ceiling of a room he shared with other students (fortunately, nobody lived above him). Norval also used the pistol to "celebrate" after he delivered his first baby as a student and for target practice at rural road signs. Word reached Dr. Vest back home in Huntington that Norval might be expelled. He, too, was not amused and sent Norval a stern letter:

> I regret exceedingly to hear that you are allowing the boyish element in your nature to get the upper hand of you, and that you are making an ass of yourself around there generally and at your work. For God's sake, if you do not have any common sense . . . let Fernie take complete charge of you and tell you what [you] have to do. . . . Please settle down and behave yourself. Remember that a man as far advanced in a profession as you are should maintain his dignity and understand at all times that he is a man and not a boy and he should put away childish things.

Several students remember another side of my father, however. A friend named John Morris lacked the money to go straight into medical school from college. He worked for a year to save enough money but became discouraged. Had my father not encouraged him, he would have given up, he told me later. When John was accepted at the Medical College of Virginia, my father lent him his microscope and books.

In the spring of 1934, after only eight months in Colcord, Fernie lost her teaching job and finally joined her husband. The school board had run out of money and could no longer pay her salary, a reflection of the nation's severe economic distress in the early 1930s. But Fernie's arrival in Richmond apparently did little to inspire Norval to study harder. His grades through his third and fourth years were pretty dismal—he received

Norval relaxing the summer after his graduation from medical college, 1937. This photograph stood on a table in the living room.

a D in neuropsychiatry, which was to become his wartime specialty. But John Morris and several other classmates remembered my father as a very bright student, one who scored near the top on medical aptitude tests. The school required students whose written exams were unsatisfactory—and some of Norval's surely were—to take an oral exam before graduation. On May 24, 1937, he received a summons from the college's dean to appear in his office at nine o'clock the following morning to be examined by the school's graduation committee. Somehow, he managed to talk his way though this ordeal and graduated with the rest of his class on June 1, 1937.

As millions of Americans knew firsthand, jobs were hard to come by in 1937, even for freshly minted medical doctors. Several of my father's classmates had difficulty finding work, but Norval obtained an internship at the prestigious Scott and White Clinic in Temple, Texas. Once again, he was on the move, leaving Huntington for another adventure. This time, my mother went with him, and that summer they awaited their first child.

On July 17, 1937, the same month that Japan invaded China, they became parents of a baby boy they named Tom Eustace Carter. According to my father, Tom was a "fine-looking, red-headed, blue-eyed boy whose features resemble practically nobody."

In Texas, Norval settled into his work and Fernie settled into motherhood. When his internship was finished, he tried to find a job back home in Huntington, but Dr. Vest warned him that there was "very little likelihood" of finding work there. "The depression," he explained, "has hit this town very hard."

Norval decided to start a private practice in Timpson, Texas, where he leased a twelve-bed hospital and clinic. It was a risky business at best—when he took over, the facility had $32.47 in cash on hand. Although he brought in plenty of patients, few of them could pay. It quickly became clear that the practice could not be sustained. In October 1938 he and his young family moved back home to Huntington. If they were going to suffer through hard times, they might as well suffer with their families and old friends.

Dr. Vest's dreary assessment of Huntington's prospects proved to be correct, and in November 1938 Norval accepted a position as a staff physician in a state hospital for mentally ill patients in Spencer, West Virginia, about 100 miles from Huntington. He became friendly with a Dr. Ford, so friendly, in fact, that I owe my middle name to him. (My family and friends almost always referred to me by both names, as Walter Ford.) However, although I bear his name, I know very little about him—not even his first name.

The state hospital position lasted only fifteen months, and in 1940 the family moved back to Huntington yet again. Finally, it seemed, Fernie and Norval could settle down and live the life they had been dreaming about since they were teenagers.

Then my father went off to war.

Norval and Fernie with friends at Nags Head, North Carolina, six months before Pearl Harbor.

Doing What Is Right

3

In early August 1942, my father gave the three of us a farewell hug and then hopped into his bright yellow Chevrolet convertible. He was bound for basic training at Camp Pickett, Virginia, near the town of Blackstone, about 60 miles southwest of Richmond. It took him ten hours to drive the 365 miles between our home and the base, but other drivers would have taken even longer. My father, much to my mother's dismay, loved to drive fast.

Blackstone in 1942 was a town of about 2,700 and a trade center for dark-fired tobacco, according to Doug Coleburn's *The Japanese Attacked . . . and Then Came Pickett*. The town dated to a pre–Revolutionary War intersection of three stagecoach roads, an area called Black's and White's Taverns, after two rival tavern keepers with the family names of Schwartz (German for "black") and White. The village was known as Black's and White's until 1885, when the citizens decided on the name Blackstone; the town was incorporated three years later. Following the outbreak of World War II in Europe, the area near Blackstone was surveyed as a potential US Army training site. Construction began only twelve days after the attack on Pearl Harbor and was unfinished when my father arrived.

The original military reservation consisted of about 48,000 acres. About 260 families—more than 1,100 people—had to give up their fine farms and other property for compensation in the range of $10–$12 per acre. Thirteen thousand workers built a reservoir, 175 miles of streets, 11 miles of railroad tracks, and a cantonment area of some 1,600 buildings. Named for the Confederate general, Camp Pickett was officially dedicated on July 3, 1942, the seventy-ninth anniversary of George Pickett's unsuccessful charge at Cemetery Ridge during the Battle of Gettysburg. The camp became the home of many US Army units, including seven combat divisions and more than 500 other units, for final training before they were shipped overseas.

My father arrived at dusk on August 10 and was astonished by what he found: a bustling, midsized city that he estimated to be home to as many as 45,000 people. The camp probably held fewer, but there was no question about its vastness. Finding his assigned unit— the 110th Station Hospital, one of many hospital units

Norval at Camp Pickett, Virginia, October 1942.

within the camp—took several hours. He had hoped to see some familiar faces among the thousands of citizen-soldiers in camp, but there were none.

His new home was a small room with a steel-framed cot, a ceiling light, and one steel chair. That spartan setting soon gained a few added touches, thanks to his gift for improvisation. He found some boards and built three shelves, grabbed an iron pipe that lay underneath the barracks and used it for what he called "the sturdiest towel rack I have ever seen," and fashioned a clothesline out of spare copper wire.

During his first few days in camp, Dad bought a life insurance policy worth $10,000.

In his first letter to my mother, after discussing details of camp life, he broke some bad news. "This

Station Hospital," he wrote, "is being trained for one thing only; and that is for foreign service." In other words, he was not going to be stationed stateside. Apparently Fernie had clung to that hope, and she took the news hard, as she indicated in her reply: "It surely was a blow to hear about the foreign service side of things. I just somehow can't help but be bitter about the whole thing, but I'm trying to not think and do all my worrying at one time."

Her bitterness dismayed my father and perhaps made him feel a little guilty about his decision to volunteer. He tried to reassure her:

> I can readily see how resentful you feel about my leaving this continent & I expect you to continue to feel badly about it 'cause I do myself. But please, sweetheart, try, try to get rid of that resentful feeling. . . . It may seem over-dramatic to assume that it is my duty to do, and that I should go, but it is better for one's peace of mind to adopt just such an attitude. Otherwise it rankles in one's innards & creates a bitterness that is unhealthy. It also makes me very sad to know you are bitter about it all. I know you are unhappy but I can stand that: I can't stand to know that you are bitter.

It must have eased his conscience to know that many of his fellow officers were also married men with children. They, too, had volunteered. They, too, believed it was their duty to leave everything and everybody they loved to defend their country, and all it stood for, from the threat on the battlefields of Europe, Africa, and Asia.

But, like my father, they were not happy to be training for war. They "put up a very cheery exterior," he wrote, "but at night they are quite restless mentally and physically."

My father did have some good news: he would be granted leave every other weekend. He would not be able to come home that often, because he would have to spend twenty hours on the road for a leave that lasted only from Saturday noon until Monday morning. But at least he would be home a few times before he was shipped overseas.

I was just over two years old at the time, and, according to my mother's letters, I had a difficult time understanding that my father could not be an everyday presence in our lives. "The boys are getting along fine, but things about 'Daddy' pop up constantly," she wrote. "Walter Ford came into my room this morning, peeped over me and said 'Where is Daddy?' & I had to explain at great length all over again."

Fernie was lucky to have a support network close at hand. My parents' relatives and their many friends in Huntington helped keep us busy and relieved some of her burdens as a single parent. Not long after my father left, when I was still demanding to know where he was, my grandmother Sapho Carter invited us to a fried-chicken dinner, which she knew I would enjoy. My grandfather took my brother and me on a pleasant, late-summer walk to the depot to see the trains as they chugged in and out of town. I held my grandfather's hand the whole time. Tom, who had just turned five, proudly told our grandparents that he would look after Mom and me while Dad was gone.

Tom and Walter Ford with their grandparents, Sapho and Eustace Carter, Easter 1942.

Fernie received a welcome distraction in early September, when one of the local junior high schools asked her if she would work as a substitute teacher. With no shortage of family members willing to mind my brother and me, she accepted. "We dropped the children off at your mother's," she wrote Norval. "I taught math & typing!! Wotta day! I didn't know head or tails of their math problems but I managed, some way." The instant soldiers of the new American army were not the only people who were asked to become experts in unfamiliar fields. "Tomorrow I am to go back & teach mechanical drawing, something I still know nothing about. . . . What is mechanical drawing, anyway?"

The excitement of being back in the classroom, away from her worries for a few hours, was dampened when my brother asked whether she was going to teach all the time and leave him behind. "I felt like saying 'to hell with teaching,'" she confessed. "If I had anybody to tell me not to do it—I'm afraid it wouldn't take long for me to decide about the whole matter." On October 5 she wrote, "I substituted down at West Jr. High last week. Had music & nothing but boys again! There ought to be a law against jr. high boys taking music—none of 'em can sing. Their voices crack on every other note so they like to spend the time throwing paper wads & airplanes around the room. I really had to get tough on 'em."

Sapho Carter was our occasional baby-sitter, sometimes for days at a time. A few words in a letter to her son captured a sense of how life in America had changed. Describing one of her favorite meals, she wrote: "Huntington any more seems so quiet. I suppose it is because of all the young men that have gone into the service. . . . I had one fine mess of squirrel & hot biscuits the other day, also some good country honey which tasted great." During her girlhood, Grandmother Sapho had used her squirrel gun to hunt down prey on her grandfather's farm, and the intervening decades had not changed her idea of a good meal.

Huntington was by no means the only small city in America that now seemed quiet and deserted. In some small towns politicians organized impromptu parades as young men marched in civilian clothes to the local rail or bus station for the journey to basic training. Bands played, veterans of past wars snapped salutes, and loved ones wept and waved. Sixteen million Americans eventually joined or were drafted into the armed services by war's end. Most of them were young men, although almost 400,000 women volunteered too. Other young and not-so-young women joined the labor force, giving rise to the heroic image of Rosie the Riveter.

For millions of citizens turned soldiers, basic training was hell itself. Dante's fiery rings had nothing on the brutal routines and outright punishments inflicted on new recruits. As an officer and a doctor, Norval was spared the worst of this initiation, but he must have witnessed some of the drills designed to whip ordinary young men into soldiers. The pain and humiliation began with haircuts, mass physical exams, and a series of inoculations. It continued on the parade grounds and in the barracks, as drill sergeants barked unfamiliar commands and swore they had never seen such a miserable collection of so-called men. The first three weeks were the worst. Civilian life and its pleasures were a memory; drill sergeants, 50-pound packs, predawn reveille, and long forced marches were the new reality. Even for an officer and a doctor, the transition had to be terribly difficult.

Less than a month after reporting for duty, Norval was named detachment commander, with responsibility for 150 enlisted men. "It entails planning their work & play for them," he explained to Fernie. His letters contain few complaints and no details of the rigors of basic training. He may have even enjoyed it, but he would have been reluctant to divulge the truth to her. He did speculate, however, on where he might be sent. Issued a mosquito net along with a lightweight cot and a gas mask, he predicted his impending deployment. "Keep it under your hat," he told her, "but it sounds sort of tropical, doesn't it?"

Although Roosevelt and Churchill had agreed on a

"Germany First" strategy in this multitheater confrontation, combat in the South Pacific dominated America's first year at war. In early April 1942, sixteen American B-25 bombers from the USS *Hornet* bombed several Japanese cities, including Tokyo. The famous raid, commanded by Lt. Col. James Doolittle, bolstered American morale at least for a time. Soon, however, the country listened with mounting horror to reports from Corregidor in the Philippine Islands, where thousands of American and Filipino troops were attempting to hold off a Japanese onslaught. Both positions eventually fell, and thousands of Americans and Filipinos headed to prison camps, never to return. On the seas the Americans and Japanese fought to a draw at the Battle of the Coral Sea in May 1942, and then the Americans inflicted a devastating defeat on the Japanese at the Battle of Midway in June. Given the attention the war in the Pacific was receiving, Norval took one look at his mosquito netting and suspected that he might be heading to the Pacific theater.

On October 17, he turned thirty-one years old. Grandmother Sapho wrote her only child a birthday letter:

> It just doesn't seem you are going to be 31 years old. . . . I still think of you as our only dear red head "boy" running in and out as you have in years gone by (when you were close enough to be home). The last two years have been such a joy for you and your dear, precious family to be able to settle down, here in your home. . . .
>
> Then comes along this terrible brutal war to snatch and take the best boys of our land, the future of tomorrow, who are giving their blood and very lives for

their country and loved ones back home. That's the hardest to bear of all. Now we all want to do everything we can to win and have peace on earth again.

I am glad we have some very great leaders, men who are courageous and stand for the right, and right will win in the end. Gen. MacArthur said in yesterday's paper he wanted the people back home in America to pray for our "boys" as that was our main hope in this great struggle for peace. Norval, please don't forget this! Wherever you are on land, or sea, in USA or abroad, that we have a God of justice, and right, and the only one to whom we can go for safety, and one to stay us, when the world seems to be tottering or held only by a thread. . . .

Still we must strive to be cheerful and do all we can for a better day. . . . Dad and I shall always "night and day" be thinking of you. Remember this. And don't forget us.

Fernie's birthday gift—a watch—and her greetings were less philosophical and more upbeat. She had spent the night before listening to Bing Crosby and Rudy Valee on her new record player and "thinking how much more I would have enjoyed 'em if you had been in the other chair across from me."

Norval claimed he had not thought much about his birthday, but two days later he and a lieutenant got a much-coveted pass and went to Richmond to hear the Philadelphia Symphony under the direction of Eugene Ormandy. It was just the kind of evening he needed to forget about the army and the war for a few hours. He sent Fernie the program notes, and next to Ormandy's name he had jotted, "Very entertaining. Seemed to control & inspire each instrument in the orchestra." Next to the listing of Stravinsky's *The Fire Bird* he wrote, "This reminded me of you. Nicely done." He did note, however, that he did not care for one of the selections—*Götterdämmerung*, by the German composer Richard Wagner. "Good technique," he said of the piece. "But I don't like Wagner so much." He would have been interested to know just how much Hitler disagreed with him.

Training at Camp Pickett was beginning to intensify. Early every morning Norval and about 200 other soldiers would be summoned from their barracks, marched to a drill field, and put through their paces. "Then perhaps we go over an obstacle course. After my first time over I thought I was done for. Damn, we crawled through pipes, jumped ditches, ran mazes, swung across a creek on a rope, ran a horizontal ladder over a creek. Oh hell. We were really worn out. More exercises in the afternoon & lectures. Also tent-pitching and ass-scratching & nose-picking." He also trained with members of medical regiment combat teams that would be deployed on the front lines in battalion aid stations. As part of his regimen, he attended lectures on topics such as map reading and watched a movie demonstrating the different sounds of weapons.

Norval was relieved that he was not put on one of the combat teams, a high-risk assignment. "It is pitiful to see the reaction of doctors assigned to [the teams]," he told my mother. "All of them are destined to be sent to battalion aid stations. . . . They have an excellent chance of never 'coming back' and every man of them knows it. All of us in the 110th Station Hospital are envied by those poor apes, & some vainly try to get into our outfit." Within a year he himself would be trying to get out of the 110th to join a combat unit.

A few days after finishing training with the medical combat teams, Norval sent Fernie a letter, dated November 11, which contained only three words: "I love you."

Fernie knew the day was coming when her husband would leave for a place she did not know and did not care to imagine, but she continued to immerse herself in the daily life of a family without its father in a town without its men. My father's chores were now hers. She made the decisions; she managed the budget. When leaks developed in the ceilings, she had to get them fixed. When the time came to hang new bathroom curtains, she had to climb on the stool.

My parents treasured every moment they had with each other during my father's leaves. After one visit, just before Thanksgiving, my mother spent a Sunday evening sitting in the den and listening to the popular radio program, *Take It or Leave It*. The previous week Norval had been sitting across from her, and they had enjoyed the show together. "I can't help thinking about how nice it was to have you sitting in the green chair & me opposite," she wrote.

She asked him to "please, please" think of something he wanted for Christmas, but he knew that this Christmas would not be a season for gift giving: "Sugar, I'm damned if I need anything for Xmas. I'll be going "over" soon & won't be able to take much stuff along.

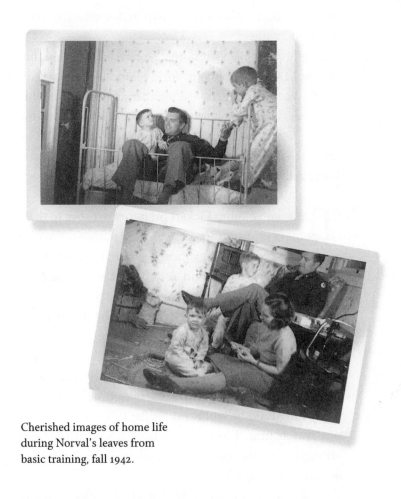

Cherished images of home life
during Norval's leaves from
basic training, fall 1942.

Most of the things I have will have to be left behind.
The only things I can think of would be (1) binoculars
(or telescope), (2) water-proof match box, (3) compass
(good one). I now know definitely that I won't be home
Xmas. I'll be coming home [November] 23rd probably,

or the 22nd. It will be my last trip in, Sweetheart, so we must make the most of it."

Before this last visit home, Norval had learned that he would ship out of New York, bound for England, in early December. I do not remember anything about his last visit. When his leave was over and it was time for him to return to Camp Pickett, we said goodbye and he waved to us from that yellow Chevrolet. We never saw him again.

The men at Camp Pickett prepared to move to their point of embarkation. Myrtle F. MacBrayer, the wife of Norval's commanding officer, wrote to the wives of all the officers in her husband's command, expressing her thanks for their sacrifice and expressing her own appreciation of their strength and character. Her letter to Fernie read in part: "I have the greatest respect for your husband and know he'll be of much help to my husband. As a special favor I have asked him to watch over my husband's health. He has so much responsibility I'm afraid he will break under it if someone does not watch him. I know somehow we shall find the strength to "carry on." It is a mighty difficult time we are going through."

Norval left Camp Pickett at eight o'clock on the night of November 28. His unit's movement was a closely guarded secret, even from fellow soldiers, so he and the other members of the 110th Station Hospital had remained out of sight all day. Under the cover of darkness, a convoy of fifteen trucks ferried the men from camp to the train station, where they boarded a special train of five Pullmans and two baggage cars. After dinner the soldiers retired to their beds and their thoughts. They rattled up the coast, toward Camp Kilmer in New Jersey, arriving just in time for breakfast.

Norval was barely installed in his barracks when he received a nice surprise: permission to visit New York City, about an hour away by bus, which he had seen only once before. He sent Fernie some candy from the city and then took in a movie starring the now-forgotten comedy team of Olsen and Johnson.

> It was magnificent. My sides are still sore due to laughing. There was only one thing keeping me from enjoying it to the fullest—and that was an undercurrent of sad loneliness—your absence. It made my throat feel mighty tight at times. However, I feel content & at peace with myself & with God. It seems to me that we are doing what is right; that we are sincerely fighting for something worth while—the right for individual peace & happiness.
>
> I'll be back to see you & the boys someday and we can all be happy again. Then we can do the things we dream about today. And I can whisper into your ear. The boys are growing very fast & I miss seeing them do it, but their being with you can only make them fine young men, which will be a delight to both of us later on.

As the staff of the 110th Station Hospital waited to be ordered aboard ships, a group of nurses arrived to join them on their journey to a new posting in England. Almost 60,000 women served in the US Army Nurse Corps during World War II—and that was not nearly enough. As Stephen Ambrose points out in *Citizen*

Soldiers, the need for nurses was so severe that a measure to draft them passed the US House of Representatives and nearly passed the Senate, losing by a single vote. These unheralded women faced the same dangers as doctors and medics, but their service was often unappreciated. According to Ambrose, 41 percent said their families were opposed to their decision to join the Nurse Corps, but for many a wounded soldier, the nurses were a blessing.

The officers of the 110th Station Hospital met the nurses at a formal reception in the camp's Officers Club, where they shared a few drinks and dances. "They seem to be a good bunch of gals & it looks as tho we'll get along O.K.," he told Mom. "Most are Southern gals but a few are Yankees." What Fernie thought about this influx of women into camp is unrecorded.

On or around December 7, the staff of the 110th Station Hospital boarded the grand cruise ship *Queen Mary* on New York's waterfront. The *Queen Mary* and its sister ship, the *Queen Elizabeth,* had been converted from luxury liners to troop ships to ferry hundreds of thousands of American soldiers from the East Coast to Great Britain.

The crossing, which took about five days, was perilous. The Battle of the Atlantic was well under way, with German submarines on the prowl for Allied ships. The *Queen Mary* sailed with an escort for the last 160 miles of the journey, but even friendly ships posed a danger. On October 2, the liner had collided with a British cruiser serving as an escort. The *Queen Mary*, which had about 10,000 American troops aboard, sliced through the escort ship near the Irish coastline, killing more than 300 of its crew. The captain, ever fearful of enemy submarines and under strict orders to continue on his journey, did not stop to rescue anyone.

Poor weather accompanied my father across the Atlantic, and at one point the *Queen Mary* "damned near capsized," he wrote. Stationed up top with an anti-aircraft battery at the height of the storm, he was amazed to see the huge ship tossed about so easily. "One moment the top deck was at its usual height (several stories, about seven, I suppose) & then, swoom! down, over, and forward she would pitch. It was magnificent! I thought for sure I'd get seasick, but didn't."

Once in England, Norval rode a troop train that took him through the English countryside, much of it bearing the scars of nearly three years of war. He even met the lord mayor of one city along the way, commenting, "I don't know which he would rather I do, kneel, or present him with one of my few chocolate bars."

The affection and hospitality of the British people genuinely moved him, especially when he caught glimpses, for the first time, of the realities of war that the British had known since 1939:

> As we traveled across the Isles the people waved and cheered our train. Their attitude was quite pitiful & it put lumps in our throats. I saw many children & I got to give one girl a chocolate bar & one boy 5 cents. These kids have it very tough but seem to be quite happy.
>
> Tell Tom & W.F. that I think of them a lot & hope to get back to you all as soon as possible. Am glad the "Jerries" haven't done to you all what they did over here.

It was Christmas, and despite the excitement and the new surroundings, Norval and his fellow soldiers could not hide their loneliness. "I never saw so many long faces," he wrote. Like hundreds of thousands of GIs, he tried to imagine what the day had been like at home. "How many times did the boys turn over the tree?" he asked. From his lonely post in England, he confided that he wished he could see us all.

A Nation of
Broken Hearts

4 Although the English people could not
have been more accommodating and
his work was interesting if sporadic, Norval was terribly
depressed and homesick. Perhaps only now, with the
war no longer a distant abstraction, did he fully appreciate the enormity of his decision to join the army. This
was not just another adventure like heading off to a new
college. Gunfire now was no foolish prank; it was deadly
business.

Norval plunged into the work of setting up a military hospital in southwest England, but his nighttime
thoughts inevitably drifted westward across the Atlantic.
Fernie's frequent letters were a sweet torture. While

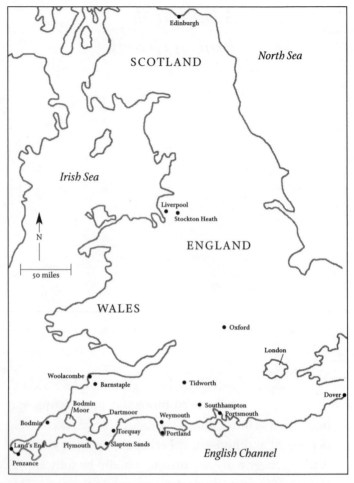

Map of England showing the locations of Norval's training sites, 1942–44.

reveling in every scrap of news about his sons, every bit of gossip about family and friends, his heart ached as he pictured all that he was missing. "I feel at times that I am hallucinating because it seems that you & the boys can be made so readily visible," he wrote to Fernie. "But it is all pantomime—no voices."

To drive away the pain of what he called his "damn gnawing homesickness," Norval drank. He had started drinking during his short stay at Camp Kilmer, New Jersey, as he awaited embarkation to England. "I was afraid to soberly face the thought of leaving you all," he later admitted. "I just couldn't stand up to it emotionally." Now, in his loneliness in England, he was drinking up to a quart of whiskey a day. Although surprised that he was able to drink that much—"evidently my tolerance increased"—he claimed that he was never drunk. "I was just anesthetized, I suppose."

Drinking was a common enough treatment for the maladies of many young American soldiers. England seemed "short on whiskey & we consume a lot of that," he noted. It was hardly social drinking, though. Norval and his friends were not going out to London's clubs and buying drinks for the young ladies of England or the brave men of the Royal Air Force. Their drinking was purely medicinal, the kind of drinking that makes pain bearable.

Even a quart of whiskey could accomplish only so much, however. "I have been feeling very homesick for several days," he wrote on February 26, 1943, not long after receiving pictures of Tom and me in front of our Christmas tree. "The depression was profound & bordered on the pathological. . . . The pictures came, & seeing those kids around the tree just about did me in. I would give anything to see you all & tell you how much I love you."

Part of Norval's problem was that his unit did not have a great deal to do, at least at first. A colleague, Dr. Norman Cannon, later explained to me that units such as the 110th Station Hospital had been designed to support the coming invasion. Until that event, there was no shortage of paperwork or short-term tasks and chores, but the doctors found little use for their professional skills. The idleness made camp life miserable. Everybody, Norval reported, was becoming "quite irritable."

In late January, he traveled to the resort town of Torquay on the Channel coast. The town had been transformed by war refugees from many of the countries Hitler had overrun. He spent hours talking with them and with the locals. He sometimes found it hard to talk to the English people—although courteous, they did not chat as freely as Americans—but he came to understand how much they had suffered while America was watching from afar: "This is a country of broken hearts. Honestly, I could never realize how much of a Hell war can be. It is very cruel. This war has destroyed much more than property and human lives. It is depressing & degrading; it has destroyed ideas and ideals; it has changed spirits & wounded souls. I wonder when the world will recover from it."

Norval had been in England for just over a month, but already he had met some of the men to whom Britain and the world owed so much: the pilots of the Royal Air Force. Their historic defense of Britain's skies in 1940 was the stuff of legend. Without their skill and courage, Hitler surely would have launched Operation Sea Lion, his planned invasion of Britain, in the fall of 1940. The

Luftwaffe never could gain control of British airspace, and in frustration Hitler turned his attention to Operation Barbarossa, the invasion of his onetime ally of convenience, Soviet Russia. Still, Hermann Göring's air force continued its terrifying bombardment of England—not just airfields and military depots, which had borne the brunt of the blitz, but also civilian targets. It was as if the Nazi monster, enraged by the wounds Britain had inflicted, was striking back in vengeance, determined only that more blood should pour into the streets of London, Coventry, and other British cities.

The RAF's mission in 1943 was more aggressive than the desperate defense it had mounted three years earlier. Pilots in single-engine Spitfires and Hurricanes continued to harass the Luftwaffe over Britain, but crews in long-range bombers now flew across the English Channel by night, bombing the very heart of the enemy while its ground forces engaged the Russians in a titanic struggle on the Eastern Front. Some of the RAF pilots flew American-made B-17s, known as Flying Fortresses. These legendary aircraft had made their RAF debut in July 1941, months before America entered the war, as part of the lend-lease agreement between the United States and Britain. The British pilots who flew them were trained by Americans.

These pilots made a strong impression on Norval. They lived for the moment, from mission to mission, knowing that their long-term chances for survival were slim. "These young, vivacious aviators are interesting to study," he noted in a detached, professional tone. "They never know whether they will 'come back' or not. Our

Fortresses are good planes, & most of them come back, but the men get badly shot up." Norval continued to work with pilots and their crews during the ensuing months. His respect and affection for these brave men must have been mutual, for in mid-March he was invited to accompany a crew on a bombing run over the Ruhr, the heart of industrial Germany and a prime target of Allied air strikes. Although tempted, he chose discretion over valor, "because of Fernie & the boys," he wrote. He had seen what happened to crew members, even on airplanes that made it home. "Arms off, some completely decapitated, some merely scratched. The boys are truly heroes. It's hell to fly a plane for several hours when the inside is splattered with the guts of a recent friend of yours."

Norval's battles with depression and loneliness during his first months in England offer a startling contrast to popular images of army life during the buildup to D-Day. Many books on the period show GIs in their dress uniforms on dance floors with pretty English girls in their arms or hoisting pints of ale in quaint British pubs. Once the GIs were no longer seen as welcome saviors or at least interesting curiosities, the British complained that the problem with the Americans was that they were "overpaid, oversexed . . . and over here." This famous phrase was partly good-natured ribbing, but it also could have a hostile, envious edge.

Norval's letters provide a far different narrative of the American soldier's experiences during Operation Bolero, the buildup of US armed forces in England. There is no talk of dances or boozy jaunts through Piccadilly Circus, only longing and loneliness: "Sweetheart, take care of yourself & remember constantly that I love you more than anything in the world. I want to sit and talk and read with you. I want to hold you in my arms and love you. I want to listen to records with you. I want to chase you about the house & toss cold water on you. I want to drive you about with the top down and make you fuss. I want to mumble in your ear. I want to see you, dear, and forget about air raids and rations and living in quarters and dammit! I want to come home."

No doubt many American soldiers, married or single, sought fleeting companionship in wartime Britain, knowing that tomorrow a bomb might land on them, an anti-aircraft gunner might turn their airplanes into fireballs, or even a routine training drill might turn deadly. But Norval resisted these thoughts and these temptations. He wrote to Fernie: "I always have [been] & always will be true to you all." His letters offer anecdotal evidence that other GIs were equally determined to remain true to their wives and sweethearts. "It is quite amusing to see how many venereal disease wards have been built in the Army hospitals over here, and nearly every one of them is empty," he wrote. The wards were nicknamed "Brown's folly," after the colonel who ordered them built.

Even as air raids became a part of his daily routine— "I . . . know how to duck when I see eggs dropping & jump for a ditch from machine-gun fire"—Norval refused to surrender his dreams of tomorrow. He told his wife: "Nothing is going to happen to me to prevent our being together again—keep that in mind. I just know everything is going to be all right."

Idleness remained the greatest curse. Work took a soldier's mind off home and family; lack of work left time to brood. In mid-March, Norval's commanding officer charged him with overseeing construction of a new hospital in Stockton Heath, Cheshire, a few miles from Liverpool. He welcomed the assignment and the increased responsibility. "I am quite pleased . . . & am glad to know the CO trusts me with it," he told Fernie. "I'll have 50 men and one other officer with me."

Conditions at the construction site were primitive at best. For several days, as construction began in earnest, Norval lived in a "mud hole." One Sunday morning he tried to relax by walking to a nearby farm and riding a frisky racehorse. But even this exercise inspired thoughts of home. Noticing "the well-rounded rump" of the horse, he wrote, "it suddenly occurred to me how nice it would be to set Tom & W.F. on there."

Perhaps because he was college educated, Norval was given some surprising assignments. Early in his Cheshire posting, he was asked to defend an army cook charged with drunkenly drawing a knife on a military policeman. Norval had no training as a lawyer, but he clearly had charm and a gift for public speaking. Although he had little doubt that his "client" was guilty, he quickly educated himself in the fine points of military jurisprudence. Perhaps he regarded this assignment as another welcome distraction or believed that every defendant is entitled to a strong defense. In any event his research uncovered technicalities that the prosecutor had overlooked. The court-martial found the cook not guilty, a verdict that left Norval somewhat confused and even embarrassed. Of his client he wrote dryly: "He shows his gratefulness in many ways, the most unpleasant is borrowing a couple of pounds off me a week or so before pay-day."

As the hospital in Cheshire neared completion, Norval found time to write to my brother, around the time he decided not to join the bombing run to Germany:

> Son, you must be growing quite a bit now & your mother tells me that you are getting to be quite a man now. It was very nice for your grandmother to write & describe how well you looked after W.F. You must be careful with him—don't correct him too much but explain to him when he is wrong. You must judge him carefully & tell him how to help mother about the house.
>
> I notice that the little English boys & girls are just like you all. They play & shout even though they have been mistreated by this war. Tom, when you see pictures of airplanes in the Saturday Evening Post & when you hear them roaring overhead, you must remember that anything so powerful & beautiful is capable of doing a lot of good for people like yourself if they are only used properly. There are some men in the world today who have been misguided and they are mis-using these airplanes. They hurt people with them. Always remember, Tom, that we must find a good use for all things & then exercise it. To do the former requires thought. To do the latter entails untiring labor.

When his work in Cheshire was finished, Norval was ordered to Oxford University for thirty days of study at the Neuropsychiatric School of the European

Theater of Operations. He left for Oxford on April 6, 1943, and was quartered in a private home about a mile from the university. His temporary hosts, an English family named Evans, delighted him by serving tea, crumpets, and scones at four o'clock every afternoon. Not long after spending nights in the "mud hole" in Cheshire, he now had his own room, a comfortable bed, a bathtub, and a bureau. He also had use of a radio and a record player belonging to his hosts' son, who was with the British army in North Africa. One night he tuned in to the Armed Forces Radio Network and heard a program featuring Bob Hope, Jerry Colonna, and other American comedians. He laughed the night away, his first good laugh in weeks. Some evenings, after he returned from work, piano music drifted into his room. His hosts' daughter played the instrument but not, he observed, as well as Fernie. "The sound of some of those songs makes me homesick. I can be here and visualize you playing with your specs halfway down your nose & me sitting in a near-by chair."

Busy in Cheshire, Norval no longer reached for the bottle when his thoughts drifted to home. His Oxford schedule brought the welcome order of routine. He had to be at the hospital, a mile away, at seven o'clock every morning, and he rose early enough to walk. There were lectures from ten until noon, a board meeting to discuss patients' cases at one o'clock, ward work until four, supper at four thirty and, every other day, a drill at six. He was in bed by seven.

It was exhausting and heartbreaking work. At Oxford were the wounded of North Africa, where a combined British-American force was battling German forces, including elements of Erwin Rommel's feared Afrika Korps. Many American generals considered the fighting in Tunisia, Algeria, Morocco, and Libya little more than nipping at the edges of the Nazi empire. In fact, before American troops landed in North Africa as part of Operation Torch in November 1942, US commanders had been pushing for a cross-channel invasion of France. Gen. Dwight D. Eisenhower gave voice to American impatience in 1942: "We've got to go to Europe and fight—and we've got to quit wasting resources all over the world and, still worse, wasting time." Churchill and the British, ever mindful of the appalling slaughter in France during World War I, favored a back-door approach—first clear North Africa, then Sicily, then Italy. Churchill himself persuaded the American generals to adopt a more cautious initial strategy.

The brutal battles in North Africa and on the beaches of Sicily in 1942, many historians agree, provided American troops with valuable combat experience—most had been civilians only a year before. North Africa also saw the emergence of one of the war's most colorful and most controversial commanders, George S. Patton.

Many Allied soldiers brought to Oxford from North Africa for treatment were wounded psychologically. During World War I, doctors had been overwhelmed with cases of men whose psyches had been brutalized by that conflict's large-scale carnage—"shell shock," they called it. During World War II, such patients were said to be suffering from "exhaustion." Generally they were treated behind the lines, in aid stations or in field hospitals; most recovered there and soon were back on the front lines. Others had to be evacuated to hospitals in Britain. Some never recovered from the trauma and were sent home, often never to emerge from the grounds of a veterans hospital. As a psychiatric physician, Norval sympathized with these men whose bodies bore none of the scars or disfigurements of war. General Patton, in contrast, was famously skeptical not only of soldiers suffering from "exhaustion" but also of doctors who recognized the mental trauma of war. In a well-documented incident during the Sicilian campaign, Patton slapped a hospitalized soldier who lay in bed in anguish over the terrors he had witnessed.

As he worked with these traumatized soldiers, Norval became angry with Americans back home who, he felt, did not appreciate the suffering he saw every day. "If the people back in the states knew what these young men are doing for freedom and liberty they would no longer think these two words sounded trite or corny," he wrote. "These fighting men really go through hell. Some get killed. Many get wounded and they all get the hell scared out of them at times. It is very pitiful and depressing."

The terrible sights and perhaps the incoherent rambling of his patients led him to write an emotional letter to my brother and me. He knew we could not fully understand what he was saying, but he wanted us to know that the images we saw in the news did not capture the horror and tragedy of war:

I am now treating men whose minds have been damaged by this war. It is another bad thing that war does. You know that some soldiers get killed in battle and some get crippled by bullets, but there are also a great number whose minds become deranged by the frightfulness of combat. They see so many unpleasant sights and experience so much danger to themselves that they are unable to use their minds as you and I do. Some of them are pretty sad and depressed and nothing is bright and cheerful for them. They are unable to look at the pretty flowers and enjoy them like you do. I remember how you boys used to run about the flowers and squat and look at them and then bend over and stick your nose in them. It's very nice to be able to do that, and I hope you always will be able to do it. I am living in an English home now. I get to see a lot of boys and girls. They ask me about you two and want to know if my sons are good boys. Of course I tell them how good you are to mind and how nice you are at the table and that you don't quarrel very much. They want to know if you are taking care of your mother & I tell them you are looking after her very carefully & help her do a lot of things & never cause any trouble. They don't have chewing gum & candy over here because of the war, but the US sends some to its soldiers. You know I don't care for it as much as these little boys do, so I give them my supply. They are very polite & say "Thank you, Sir." Then they run & divide it with their playmates.

On the night of April 23—Good Friday, 1943—as his Oxford assignment neared conclusion, Norval was awakened by the sounds of nearby anti-aircraft fire. He dressed quickly and ran outside, squinting into the cloudy sky for a glimpse of German bombers. He saw none until a single German fighter plane—a Focke-Wulf 190D, a swift aircraft that reached speeds of 435 miles an hour—suddenly swooped down. For an awful moment he thought he was doomed, but the pilot, apparently lost, did not fire. As the plane zoomed through the air, British gunners lit up the sky with shells.

My father's letters to Tom and me emphasized the horror of war but in language that would not frighten us. There are no tales of heroics and glory, only a palpable sense that although the war was necessary, it inflicted terrible sufferings on innocent people, even children. And he assured us that all people, even those we were fighting, wished only for an end to the death and destruction.

Like his descriptions of the gloomy realities of camp life, my father's gentle and humane messages to us were very different from the popular images at home. The idea that our enemies hated the war, just as we did, was almost subversive. Newspapers, magazines, and radio programs depicted them as ruthless and evil—and, of course, their cause surely was. But the letters asked Tom and me to think of the enemy not as a faceless entity but as a collection of people not so different from us.

> There are soldiers of many nationalities over here and they have pretty colored uniforms. However, I am sure we shall all be happy when the pretty uniforms are replaced with civilian peacetime clothes. The soldiers are handsome in peacetime but it is an ugly thing they have to do in war. Remember that most human beings

really don't want to kill each other. The Germans, Italians, and Japanese soldiers have the same feelings about war that you & I have and will probably be glad when it is over.

Although it is clear how my father felt about war in general, he believed not only that this one was necessary but also that people at home, particularly politicians, could do more to support the GIs. He was particularly angry that some political leaders were resisting the military's plan to build an army of millions to defeat the combined Axis powers. This tension between military and political leaders is as old as the nation itself. To the frustration of George Washington and his top generals, many influential members of the Continental Congress believed that the Revolutionary War could be fought without a large standing army, which many politicians considered a danger to democracy. Standing armies also were expensive, so the politicians' preference was for part-time militia units that could be called up when necessary. The revolution's military leaders saw matters differently and constantly requested more troops in the regular army.

As the buildup in England continued in the late spring of 1943, Norval vented his frustration:

I . . . saw that some members of Congress were against the War Department's demand for such a large army. Those men should be enlightened or shot. We shall need a much larger force than we have now. We are up against some tough armies. The successes (costly) in [North Africa] shouldn't deceive people. We are up against only a very small enemy force there. On the continent there are many divisions of well-equipped men. We shall need an enormous gun-power to flatten it. One can't have a great gun-power without having a great number of men. . . . People in the states better wake up & get to work. It makes us very much ashamed when such news gets over here & we have to listen to it at the same time we see the great output of effort & materials and the great fighting spirit of the British.

Norval began to feel that when this mass of men and materiel was ferried from England to France he wanted to be on the front lines. In late May 1943 he was detached from the 110th Station Hospital for several weeks to serve alongside the men of the Twenty-ninth Infantry Division in southwest England, an assignment he believed could lead to front-line duty as the leader of a neuropsychiatric team. This possibility, which Norval mentioned casually in a letter, frightened Fernie. No doubt she had taken comfort in knowing that her husband was in a relatively safe army hospital in England and perhaps had assumed that he would remain there for the war's duration. His growing expertise in neuropsychiatry seemed like work that would be performed far from the battlefield itself. Why, she wanted to know, would the army post psychiatric teams on the front lines? Dad explained that "it was the most advantageous place. . . . Acute psychoneuroses (70–80 percent) can be cured within 48 hours at the front. But if they are allowed to get back to the rear echelons most don't recover for months and sometimes retain their troubles for keeps."

He actually underestimated the percentage of cases "cured" at the front. During the European campaign of World War II, about 90 percent of soldiers suffering from combat stress were returned to service after immediate treatment near the front lines. Only the worst cases were sent back across the Channel for hospital treatment, and, as he suggested, many of those never recovered.

Realizing that Fernie was now even more anxious about him, Norval tried to reassure her: "I don't know whether I'll be assigned [to the front lines] or not. One never knows what will happen. I can't kick and I will do my best wherever I go. And the future doesn't worry me at all. I know everything will be all right. I have never lost my self-confidence either in regards to the present situation or to the post-war period. You & I will enjoy life again, in a more livable world, & Tom and Walter Ford will have many advantages, & we shall be proud of them."

His letter may have reassured Fernie slightly, but Norval found himself becoming fascinated with combat training and exercises and drawn to the men of the Twenty-ninth, who were preparing for the great battle to come. "They are fine looking fellows, lean, hard, alert & quick in movement and very, very serious," he reported. "There are occasional pranks & jokes in the Army but I often think how serious everyone seems to be—all military. But then one can't expect men to remain fun-seeking & light-hearted and still be able to coldly shoot and knife other men to death." Some of the officers carried "wicked-looking knives," which they hurled with great precision into target dummies. "An army of fighting men is a tremendous spectacle and quite awe-inspiring," Norval wrote to his parents.

The contrast to his descriptions of his hospital routine, filled with complaints about idleness and red tape, is striking. Although he did not transfer to the Twenty-ninth Division for another ten months, this assignment may have convinced him that this was the work he ought to be doing. Decades later, Dr. Cannon, another doctor at the 110th Station Hospital, told me that my father stood out from his colleagues because he seemed so eager to do something other than file paperwork and see the occasional patient. "Usually, most of us were perfectly happy to be in a safe unit like the 110th," Cannon wrote in 1997. "No one was shooting at us and bombing by the Germans was remote and infrequent. I, for one, was not going looking for trouble. The war was a temporary affair, noble, heroic, unique, but after all, temporary, and when it was over, I intended to go home and practice my medical specialty. Norval wanted more."

Conditions in the new camp seemed pleasant enough, with even a hint of home: "There are some hills contoured like ours, maple trees and rhododendron. The air is quite spicy & invigorating. It's still quite cool in the day & cold after 6 o'clock. There are many Hawthorne trees in bloom. They have small, delicate leaves and a white cluster-bloom similar to spiraea. They are very fragrant. It rains lightly & frequently here but mostly the sky is very blue and the clouds have a delicious grey & white fluffiness about them. A peculiar lighting effect is apparent most of the day, which is hard to describe. I appreciate this beauty, but my God I'd like to be home!"

Although the countryside was peaceful most of the time, battlefield training often spoiled the effect of the rolling hills and blue skies as airplanes practiced evasion tactics high in the English air and armored units worked on their shelling. "Peaceful, ain't it," Norval commented.

He went out with the troops into the field, observing how they lived and worked together and studying the hardships they suffered during their intensive and dangerous training exercises. This allowed him, he said, to "study neuropsychiatric problems now and anticipate what to expect in the future."

The division's location was not unknown to the Luftwaffe. "Some Gerry planes came over & strafed a certain place the other day," he wrote on May 26. "Killed 6 of our men. However, this is all very tame [compared] to what will come off in the future."

At night, even in such an active camp with serious business under way, the loneliness returned. With the day's work done and few other distractions in the English countryside, Norval's thoughts—no doubt the thoughts of everyone in camp—wandered home. He longed for the day when he would take off his uniform and resume the life he loved in Huntington. Sometimes those dreams seemed heartbreakingly real. As he lay dozing in a chair one night, he heard Fernie's voice, repeatedly calling him to the dinner table. It was one of the games they played with each other: She would call him, he would remain in his chair in the living room, and then she would have to use more persuasive tactics. The vision was fleeting, and he snapped back to consciousness, but the sensation was so real:

> I could smell steak & fried potatoes just as plainly, & that odor & mental picture still lingered for several minutes afterward. I was terribly homesick the rest of the evening. I can remember how I used to persist in sitting to get you riled up & come after me. You would pull & tug & pound me over the head & shoulders & finally kiss me on the neck with your soft lips & send shivers up my spine. Then I could goose you in the tail and kiss you & wander in to eat. Damn! Those were happy days, weren't they, Sugar? Tell the boys I love them a lot. I think of you & them constantly.

On May 28, while Norval and another officer, Colonel Root, were inspecting the aftereffects of an explosion near training camp, they spied coming toward them a shiny buggy pulled by a well-trained, well-groomed pony. Holding the reins was an elderly man wearing a brown-and-white tweed suit, a green-gray wool shirt with a white collar, highly polished brown shoes, and a frayed tweed cap over his balding head. He was Sir Henry Hoare, eighty years old, who lived with his wife, Lady Hoare, in nearby Albert Towers, a 200-year-old castle. Seated alongside Sir Henry was his land overseer, equally well dressed; in the back of the buggy, his legs dangling over the side, was one of Sir Henry's staff. Norval noticed that when the buggy stopped, the man in the back jumped off and remained ten paces away from Sir Henry, always standing at attention.

The two Americans and the English aristocrat exchanged greetings. Norval's enthusiastic handshake apparently startled and amused the reserved older gentleman, who muttered something my father could not hear, except for one word: "Americans." Dad, ever the model representative of American informality, offered Sir Henry some Fig Newtons and some peanuts. He declined but, displaying some wartime spontaneity of his own, invited the two to lunch later that afternoon. Norval and the colonel eagerly accepted.

All over England in the summer of 1943 Americans and Britons were getting to know each other in ways never imagined. The British were astonished by the Americans' informality and idealism; Americans were impressed with the Brits' stoicism, courage, and love of history. Lunch at Albert Towers that day must have been one of the most fascinating encounters of 1943: E. Norval Carter of Huntington, West Virginia, and Colonel Root of Pittsburgh, Pennsylvania, guests of Sir Henry and Lady Hoare, owners of a castle and a 1,500-acre estate, which was home to three villages and as many lakes.

My father later wrote that he had never seen a more beautiful place in his life. Near the castle were Druid ruins dating to pre-Roman times. Ancient oak and beech trees rose almost a hundred feet into the air. Peacocks strutted about the estate's meadows. Honeysuckle bushes were everywhere, as were "azaleas like I have never seen. Some were pink and rose, others were yellow, orange, orchid and purple." The building's facade looked weather beaten, however, and "had considerable fungus growth on it."

Rushing a bit because they were late, Norval and Colonel Root made their way up one of the many marble-stepped entrances and were escorted into the "minor" breakfast room, which was, he reported, "larger than the whole down stairs of our house." The castle had sixty rooms. The walls were lined with marble statues and filled with oil paintings. The furnishings were Chippendale.

Sir Henry introduced his guests to his wife, a tall, stately woman who was two years older than he but looked a decade younger. Lady Hoare was dressed in a navy blue, floor-length dress with a tightly fitted waist and wore "a funny corset that shoved her breasts upward & outward. The neck was covered by heavy, thick lace. Her hair was black with some gray." Norval noticed that a hairpin had come loose from that black mane and was hanging on the back of her dress. Gallantly removing the offending pin, he boldly took the opportunity to tighten three other hairpins, which "looked like they were made of barbed-wire without the barbs."

Lady Hoare had a crush on him, he decided—"as all old women do." Had she chosen to express her affection, however, he probably would not have been able to understand her. She had false teeth that "clanked & clunked & slipped loose on the consonants. This necessarily interrupted her conversation while she rearranged them behind a handkerchief." The Americans politely pretended not to notice.

After a delightful lunch, Norval presented Sir Henry and Lady Hoare with a token of his appreciation: a box of—what else?—Fig Newtons. Her ladyship, who had never heard of them, asked Norval if they were good for her. He could not resist, and taking Lady Hoare aside he told her, with a straight face, that as a doctor he would recommend Fig Newtons because they would help "work her bowels." Fascinated, Lady Hoare confided that she often suffered from constipation, and Norval mentioned that he occasionally had the opposite problem. "The old gal really let her hair down," he wrote, "and one could readily tell that she was certainly not in the habit of talking about such subjects." No doubt with a sly smile, she told him that "the Right Honorable Lady Blythestone had the same trouble"— loose bowels—"& she took some kind of brew for it." He wrote: "Deciding that I had better get off the bowel subject, I approached the other end of the alimentary tract by telling her to soak the Fig Newtons in her mouth a bit before chewing them. Otherwise, she would have difficulty with her dentures. She confided the obvious fact that she frequently had such trouble." Valiantly trying not to smile, he recommended an American product called Klutch. Lady Hoare seemed most grateful for the advice.

Norval had a wonderful time at the luncheon, later regaling his friends back at camp with details of his encounter with British aristocracy. The two irreverent American officers "joked about . . . having been in the Hoare house."

The afternoon with the Hoares was just one touching and amusing episode in a larger social experiment under way in Britain's towns and cities. Although the collision of Yankee soldier and reserved Brit often left both suffering from culture shock, the GIs actually had encountered something similar in basic training. After all, the war had thrown together the sons of immigrants from Brooklyn with the sons of farmers from Missouri with the sons of loggers from Oregon. In an age before regional customs and accents gave way to homogenized mass culture, an English lord probably seemed no more foreign to a West Virginian than did his army buddy from the streets of South Boston.

By the end of summer, Norval had had his fill of England. It was not home, and he resented it. "You know, Fernie, in the past, I always felt that someday you and I would visit England, but I don't feel that way any more," he wrote. "It's pretty & interesting, I suppose, but I never want to set foot here again. All that I want to do is never let you out of my sight again and stay home. Goddam, but home means a lot more to me now. It means you, the boys, carpets, curtains, chairs, electric lamps, and peace of mind. I want to listen to our records & radio, drink my whiskey, smoke my pipe, read my books, and love my wife. Yes, home means a lot to me now. It is a composite of ourselves, Sugar, & I never want it disturbed again."

It meant the world to him to hear that my brother and I remembered him and asked about him. "Tom & W.F. won't forget me I feel sure—'cause I think of them all the time. I hear their little feet on the floors and their shouts and cries and well, we will see each other again. It will be so. Their patter will become more sturdy then and I will have missed some of their babyhood, but they are still my sons & there is still a lot of time ahead."

Tom and Walter Ford beside Norval's yellow Chevy convertible, considered practically a member of the family, spring 1943.

Returning to his regular duties with the 110th Hospital Station in Stockton Heath, Cheshire, Norval was promoted to captain in late June 1943. Although pleased, he was also disappointed that few of his colleagues in military hospitals were similarly rewarded. Promotions, he noted, were a sore point everywhere in England that summer. They were too slow and too few, many officers believed, grumbling that their colleagues at home were promoted faster than they were. With the captain's bars came a pay increase of $50 a month. As a first lieutenant, Norval had earned about $300 dollars a month. He invested $10 per month in war bonds; the rest of his raise was added to Fernie's monthly allotment, which now came to about $250.

A newly promoted Captain Carter at Stockton Heath, Cheshire, one of the 110th Station Hospital's locations, July 1943.

At about the same time, he was given a new commanding officer at the 110th Station Hospital. His original commander, Col. Reuben A. MacBrayer, was relieved of his post in early July after an altercation with a junior officer. Summoned to headquarters, Norval was asked about MacBrayer's abilities as a leader and a doctor. "I had to say some very bad things about him," he wrote, "but in justice to the 'old boy' I told him all the good things I knew." The good must have outweighed the bad, because MacBrayer was transferred to an administrative position rather than discharged (he later thanked my father profusely for his support). The new commanding officer, Maj. Theodore Golden, arrived in mid-July.

Under the new regime, Norval assumed additional responsibilities. He was placed in charge of admittances and discharges, named the hospital's registrar, and given the title of commander of the detachment of patients. These tasks meant lots of desk work—just the kind of assignment for which he had little patience. He was a doctor, and he wanted to work with patients. But now he had to deal with paperwork—*army* paperwork.

Life at station hospitals like his continued to be tedious during the long prelude to the invasion of France, which was still a year away, and the commanding officer had to find creative ways of keeping the staff busy until their services were needed. Even with his new duties at the hospital, Norval's work was considerably less exciting than his weeks of observing combat training and took a toll on his psyche. He was depressed again, he told Fernie, and was avoiding his colleagues; he was even negligent in writing home. He tried going to church but found no comfort there. "I am just plain miserable," he wrote. "Work doesn't take you off my mind, although it is a help. If I had a chance to get back, I'd go AWOL & stand court martial. I want to see the boys so badly."

On a moonlit Saturday night in July 1943, Norval put on his overcoat (summers in southwest England were chillier than in West Virginia), left his quarters, and sat outside until two o'clock in the morning. He was alone but not lonely, he said—the full moon inspired memories that kept him company as Saturday night turned to Sunday morning:

> Fernie, I remembered when we first kissed. We were in the front-porch swing and you wore a lacy, fluffy something or other and your hair was so fragrant. God! How I have loved you ever since. I look back & see what a heel I have been at times. How difficult I was. What a poor excuse for a father & husband—always out on calls, then coming in & griping like hell. You were always ready to listen and agree & be sympathetic—not overly so, but as mutely as only you can do & be a master at it. I hope we don't change much while we are apart, for even a little bit of change would to me be a tragic loss. I want to go on loving you as you are & have been. Fernie, to me you are precious, priceless & something unattainable as just you yourself & not in any other person or commodity. I have at last realized something which I have long suspected: that our love is different from many; that I could never be happy with any other woman. There is only you and our product, a possession that is indescribable. Tom & Walter Ford have become a vision to me. They are like a current of air that has taken on form, and color, and sound. Whenever I picture them I seem to see them from behind plate-glass—their mouths & hands can be seen moving but their sounds are muffled, just barely audible. It warms me to think of you all, because it seems that the image is always in a warm, buoyant setting, never is it cold, dark, or heavy. And that is certainly a contrast to what I am living in over here. But then maybe our lot is better than many, for we do have our memories, trust, respect, and love. Maybe we shall

be better individuals & better peoples after this war. For as war is a hardship & trial, so do people become strengthened and tempered and learned by such impositions. Perhaps we shall be more charitable in our viewpoints and more understanding & forgiving of the weaknesses & meanness in others more unfortunate than ourselves. Little do we (over here) realize how much we are learning, but I do believe that most of us will be better citizens when we get back home. I certainly hope we shall be better daddies and husbands, for most of us realize that there has been room for improvement. I shall appreciate the privilege of being with the boys & helping them [solve] their problems. I shall miserly count every kiss you give & treasure it away.

While my father may have entertained fantasies of going AWOL to get home to us, some miserable soldiers sought a desperate way out. On a Saturday in early August, a lieutenant colonel in the Army Air Force was brought to the hospital with a gunshot wound to the chest, which Norval saw was self-inflicted. The colonel was "quite depressed & blue." They were kindred spirits, together in an army hospital.

In his official medical report, Norval wrote that the wound was the result of a line-of-duty accident. That falsehood spared the colonel a court-martial—and perhaps a death sentence. Norval's conscience was untroubled. In a confrontation between his military duties and his chosen profession of medicine, the doctor in him always overruled the captain. He conceded that he was not "being a good officer, perhaps, but I just can't get the 'civilian doctor' out of me, and I hope I never will. You know we are supposed to be officers first and doctors second, and rather stern ones too, but I am not built that way. It has earned me some criticism (and some praise) for being what I call humane."

Just the day before, a major had criticized my father for being too solicitous of his patients, even complaining that the hospital chairs were too comfortable. Norval fired back at the major "with both barrels." Nevertheless, he conceded, the chairs probably would have to go.

The coastline of southwest England was being transformed into a stage for rehearsing the Allied landing. Several thousand British civilians were forced to evacuate their homes and farms as troops and equipment arrived in vast numbers. Soldiers, tanks, and camps replaced townspeople, villages, and farms. Engineers recreated the defenses Hitler had built in France, and soon pillboxes, mined obstacles, and other defensive works dotted the once-peaceful beaches along the coast. In mid-August 1943 Norval and the staff of the 110th Station Hospital were redeployed to the southwest—to Fremington, near Barnstaple in north Devon. The men of the Twenty-ninth Division, whom he had observed during combat training earlier in the summer, were already in the area, having moved from Tidworth to Devon and Cornwall in May.

The training was intense and sometimes deadly. In late September Norval watched the Twenty-ninth Division practice landings at Woolacombe on the Bristol Channel coastline. "It was very interesting but blood chilling," he wrote. "They came in from the sea & assaulted concrete pill boxes." Veterans of the North

African and Sicilian campaigns supervised the landings—"they really know their stuff." After the exercises were finished for the day, he found some shell splinters, empty cartridges, and other evidence that these rehearsals spared no detail. Collecting a few souvenirs from the beach, he mailed them home to us. A few days later he found a stray bayonet belonging to a soldier who had drowned during a practice landing; my father sent that home, too.

The routine at the 110th Station Hospital had intensified as well. Rarely did Norval complain of idleness now. His quarters were rudimentary at best—"we live practically out of doors," he said—and uncomfortable. The staff rose before dawn, ran naked to the latrines about 10 yards away from their sleeping quarters, washed, dressed, and then rode their bicycles to the mess hall. "It takes us about 10–15 minutes to get up & get to breakfast," he wrote. "We really move fast & furiously, cussing each other, shoving, pushing, yelling & throwing water, etc." He was becoming lean and tough: his clothes were fitting more loosely, and his body was "pretty hard."

Fernie, meanwhile, was ill during much of the summer and early fall of 1943. Norval suspected an allergy but acknowledged that "there is one big factor that is being overlooked." Emotional trauma, he said, was contributing to her poor health. He had some blunt advice:

> You must snap out of it. Remember how much I love you, & laugh about it. Laugh uproariously! Grab your belly, fall on the bed and roll & laugh like Hell. Raise

the roof off the house! Scream! Pound the walls. Yell &
scream. It will really do you some good. You haven't
given vent to your emotions for a long time You have
never raised your voice, except just a little bit to say,
"Norval, don't you do that" and stamp your foot a little
bit. Loosen up a bit. Yell "Shit & Shinola" real loudly
and kick up a stink. I believe it really would help you,
Sugar.

The irony of this advice was not lost on him. After
offering his prescription for happiness, he added a
postscript: "Now you write me back & ask me why I
don't do the same thing." Sometimes Norval did take
his own advice. As he listened to a jazz version of "The
Flight of the Bumble Bee," he "got off a good scream
. . . and ran around the officer's lounge & hurdled a
couple of sofas. . . . Someone muttered fleeting & sub-
dued innuendoes about 'where are the keys?' and
'behind bars.' But I feel better now. I have been wanting to yell for a long time."

Norval also had some advice for his mother, who
was keeping Tom and me quite a bit. Apparently my
grandmother thought Tom's friends were a class be-
neath that of a doctor's son and were worried that Tom
would hear bad language and perhaps develop bad
habits. My father disagreed profoundly. How it must
have disturbed him—how powerless he must have
felt—to read that his children were being reared in what
he saw as a benevolent cocoon, but a cocoon nonethe-
less. Norval wanted his children to see life as it really
was, to see people as they really were. But he was in
England and preparing for combat. He could only

request that his parents, particularly his mother, abide by his wishes:

> Don't be so particular about Tom's health & his associates. . . . Leave him alone. He may get sick a few times, but that won't hurt him nearly as much as the mental trauma of constant care. I have seen & am seeing the results of such training in the soldiers over here. Don't think that he is too good to play with any boy; I don't care how mean he may be. Fernie will see that he gets the proper moral & cultural training under our own roof & in school. Let him see life as it really is when he is playing outside. How else can he learn to discriminate between good & bad? . . . I want him to hear people cuss & say bad things, I want him to hear people pray and sing, I want him to see dirty alleys & pretty gardens, I want him to experience combats, black eyes & bloody noses, and I want him to experience friendship, esprit de corps, & "pal around with the gang." I know that you wish to protect them and you feel this to be right. But it just isn't, Mom. "Protection" should be the aim to strengthen their minds and bodies, so they will acquire "know-how." Let them out & run wild.

As Norval's thirty-second birthday approached and fall arrived in the English countryside, there was reason to celebrate. The Allies had cleared North Africa and Sicily of Axis forces, Mussolini had been overthrown, and Italy had surrendered. The Nazis denounced the Italians as traitors to the Axis cause, and German troops marched into Rome and other Italian cities to await the next stage of the Allied advance— an invasion of Italy. These victories led Norval, and no doubt many other soldiers, to hope that the end was near. He told Fernie that he believed they would be together again in 1944.

On October 17, his birthday, he wrote another touching letter to Fernie, saying that his only wish was a kiss from her:

> Sweetheart, I miss you so damned much: your voice, your hair, your eyes, your touch, you. If we could only see each other for a little while, how wonderful it would be! I want to kiss you and hug you and tell you how much you mean to me. What shall we do when we get together again? Where shall we go? How will we make up for lost conversation & exchange of ideas? There is one big consolation, and that is the way we feel toward each other. The way we understand one another. That is our most valued possession. Every time I sit quietly for awhile all sorts of conversations pass through my mind. It's been a long separation now but your picture never dims. It's funny how one's thoughts run—it looks as tho memories would fade, but they don't. It is not often that I recall definite things in our past, instead there is a constant imaginary present that exists all the time. I see the house, the yard, the rooms, the boys, the radio, the toys, and all. But it isn't as tho it were several months ago. It is right now. That is quite a comfort. But when the blues come on & I am by myself, then the past comes up. Those blues & spells of depression come all too frequently now. It is hard to stand. I'll never be able to adjust to being away from you. I have long ago found out how much you mean to me. You are the most important influence I have. All my thinking & decisions are colored by your thinking and your attitudes. How would Fernie like this, or how would Fernie do that? I know I haven't been as good an officer as one

should be because I can't keep my mind wholly on my work—I constantly have HOME bobbing up in my mind. . . . And I am glad that it is so. Miserable? Yes, but I would have it no other way. I take pleasure in realizing that sadness is present because it makes me realize how valuable you & your influence are to me. Without that life would be so dull. When all this is over and we are together again I believe I shall be glad it happened. It has crystallized an insight & results in a realization that should be prized by us both. How else could we be made so acutely aware of the fact that we loved each other so much? That we were so much a part of each other? Never before did I realize the full significance of the oft repeated poetry & prose about two lovers being "as one." I see now that it is not pretty, empty phraseology. It is something vital! It is real. And it is marvelously beautiful. It is a blending of love, thoughts & ideas, manners, tastes, likes & dislikes, and also a physical bonding. The blending is probably not complete. I suppose it is a continuous, never-ending process. But what has occurred in the past is enduring & permanent. We shall never be separated spiritually. Only loss of mental faculties in both could wipe-out its existence, and I wonder if that would do it? How much will each of us have changed when we are once more together? I realize that I have a "harder" and "sterner" attitude than formerly. I realize that military life has & will continue to change me. You will be changing too but not along the same lines. You will have to help me overcome a lot when I get back, because my changes are probably not for the best. I try & not let myself become as too many officers are becoming, but it is hard to walk though a dust storm & not become dusty. I hope it can someday be brushed off. You brush the part of me that I can't reach. Will you, Sugar?

When the American commanders first began planning Operation Bolero—the buildup of American forces in Britain—they had hoped that 1943 would see a massive Anglo-American invasion of Hitler's Fortress Europe. But the North African and Sicilian campaigns had dashed those hopes and made it clear that any such invasion would have to wait until mid-1944. Some Americans privately wondered if Churchill and the British truly supported the idea of a cross-Channel invasion. During World War I, Churchill, then first lord of the admiralty, had supported a plan to break the deadlock on the western front by attacking Germany from the south, from Turkey. The result was the disaster at Gallipoli, where Allied troops were slaughtered and the invasion force was forced to withdraw.

Now, more than a quarter century later, Churchill seemed to be repeating the mistake of his youth as he pushed the Allies to attack what he called the "soft underbelly" of Nazi Germany: Italy and the Balkans. Hitler's Fortress Europe was concentrated along the English Channel and on the North Sea Coast, the most likely site of the expected Anglo-American invasion, whereas Italy and the Balkans had no such defenses. The American generals, however, believed that the application of overwhelming force against an opponent's main defenses was the quickest way to end the war, the fastest route to Berlin.

As 1943 drew to a close, it was clear that although the Allied invasion would not take place that year, it was only months away. Training continued to intensify, and Norval saw the results firsthand. In late October four critically wounded men—"booby-trap cases," he called them—were admitted "one after another." They "are in shreds but I believe they will live. Their eyes and hands caught hell." The hospital also saw an increase in combat neuroses. "Some are very severe & pathetic," he reported. Among those sent to his care was a homosexual soldier, who was being treated as if he were suffering from mental illness. The hospital staff itself was not immune to stress, tension, and loneliness—one of Norval's fellow medical officers had to be admitted to another army hospital for treatment for severe depression.

It certainly did not help that my father had grown to dislike his new commanding officer. "I have had about all I can stand," he wrote on November 11. Some of Norval's friends had been transferred to other units and, he noted enviously, seemed a great deal happier to be away from the 110th Station Hospital. "There is talk that a lot of shifting about will be done," he wrote. "I hope they do transfer me to a field unit. I have seen a lot of Army hospitals and am plenty disgusted. The happiest soldiers & officers we see are from the field."

When Norval was away from the hospital—away from the paperwork, the red tape, and his commanding officer—he felt useful and happy. He was sent to the coast again to observe rehearsals of beach assaults, observations conducted not from afar but in the landing craft with the troops. "It's a thrilling thing to come in on an assault craft and pour out in a hurry," he wrote. "The water is cold as hell but it is invigorating. When I finished up over there I could taste powder, smoke & grit sand in my teeth."

Sensing that he needed a change, if only a brief one, Norval asked for and received a seven-day leave in mid-November. He took a train to London and then to Edinburgh. The possibility of a more permanent change, to a field unit preparing for duty on the front lines, was very much on his mind. Clearly, as his letters show, he admired the soldiers of the Twenty-ninth Division, and this admiration was not one-sided; the men he treated respected his professionalism and his devotion to their care. Victor Pedriera, a sergeant assigned to the Twenty-ninth and one of my father's patients, had written him a thank-you note in October: "Well, Captain, I pray and hope we meet again. . . . To me you're just like a Dad. I wish there were more of you all. Maybe things would be different."

On returning to hospital duty, Norval was confronted with yet more tedious work. "We are running over our bed capacity," he wrote. "I haven't caught up & I have worked to mid-nite to do so. Then there was training schedules to arrange and a lot of other . . . red-tape to be worked on." He hinted that a change might occur, although he phrased it in a way that suggested he was not actively seeking a transfer. "I think I may be placed with a combat unit," he said. "I would welcome the change to get with Army Ground Forces because this CO of ours is typical of the whole [hospital service] over here—stinko." In a follow-up letter, addressed to "Fernie & Apes," he reassured my mother that if he were transferred to field duty, it would be "just as safe . . . as anywhere." This was a dubious statement, but perhaps she took some comfort from it. "I know I would be happier there than where I am now, even if it is more muddy."

Norval, of course, knew the truth. Field duty was dangerous work, even in training. In mid-December he once again joined the soldiers of the Twenty-ninth Division to practice beach landings. He and a colleague were in a landing craft in rough seas when another vessel capsized, throwing the crew with their weapons and heavy equipment into the sea. Norval and his friend tried to rescue a soldier hanging on to a life preserver, but the sea swept him away. Seven soldiers died in training accidents in thirty-six hours. Yet the training area was precisely where he wanted to be.

The invasion was approaching. Norval explained to Fernie that H-Hour was the time fixed for the initial landings, which would take place on D-Day, the day of the assault. "'D' isn't very far off, Sweetheart," he wrote.

It was Christmas in England, but there was little joy among the hundreds of thousands of soldiers in the training camps of southern England. The GIs knew that they would soon be ordered to their points of embarkation, where an armada would take them across the English Channel to France. Awaiting them would be the most formidable defenses that the German army could assemble. Behind the German front lines were mobile panzer divisions poised to race to the invasion beaches and prevent a breakthrough. Few soldiers have felt the burden of history as did these GIs from West Virginia, the Bronx, South Dakota, and the Pacific Northwest, an amalgam of cultures, regions, accents, religions, and ethnicities, all subordinate to the uniforms they wore—the uniforms of the United States armed services.

As the holiday approached, Norval told Fernie that he was happy to learn from her letters that I remembered him. I was three and a half years old, and my father had been away for more than a year—a lifetime to a child my age. "I am glad that W.F. remembers me, 'cause I am scared that he will forget me," he wrote. "I know Tom won't but W.F. was so young and irresponsible when I left. He will always be irresponsible, I believe, and I hope. He will be less affected by the unpleasant things of life than Tom will be. . . . Maybe he will change, but I think not."

On Christmas Eve, Norval wrote a bittersweet letter home, describing how he and some other GIs spent the day:

> We have been very busy today and this afternoon we entertained about 200 English children, many of whom are war orphans. They ranged from diaper age to 13 years old. My we had fun—more so than the children. At least we had a deeper enjoyment, and that can't be called "fun," I suppose. I couldn't stay at the party, though: I am too chicken-hearted. They reminded me of too much. Thank God one little blue-eyed girl with red cheeks urinated on my field jacket. That helped the day a lot. The kids were, well, just kids. Like any the world over. Some showed evidences of avitaminosis—mild. But damn they were wonderful. We fed them the best food we could get out of Supply and gave them our candy rations which we had saved for the past month. The boys & girls were really bewildered & thankful. One little boy stuffed some gum & candy in

his pockets & I asked him what he was doing. He said his sister was sick in bed but as soon as she got well he would give it to her. Can you beat that? And only 10 years old! Most of these kids are very thoughtful & kind. Nearly all are very polite. I left and went to my ward. One private had a guitar & with his help we got everyone singing. Everyone is lonesome & homesick. The nurses are grand to try to cheer everyone up. One of them is taking me to a Catholic High Mass tonight at midnight. She insists it will do me good. I don't believe it, but I shall go.

His thoughts, of course, drifted home on that magical night of memories:

I can see you fixing trees & wrapping presents & trailing things all about, & then winding up with a beauti-

Tom and Walter Ford sending greetings to their dad, Christmas 1943, and prompting Norval's query: "Why did they salute with their left hands?"

ful arrangement. My—I would give anything to be sitting there on the floor with you & occasionally reaching over & blowing in your ear. I hope the boys will be happy in the a.m. I know you won't be entirely so. I opened your package tonight & got into the Hershey bars. They are wonderful. But Goddammit, it is sad, isn't it?

Fighting for
a Way of Living

5

Norval was dropping hints to Fernie.

He had made up his mind that he could no longer tolerate life in the 110th Station Hospital. The more he saw of the Twenty-ninth Division, the more he longed to be part of something greater and, in his eyes, more noble than the relatively humdrum life of an army hospital. The day of the great invasion was nearing, and he wanted to be part of it.

He could not bring himself to tell Fernie what he was planning to do—request a transfer to a medical field unit with the Twenty-ninth Division. By the end of 1943, the division knew it was going to play a critical role in the D-Day assault. Just how important that role would be remained unknown, at least to the rank-and-file soldier, but there was little doubt that somebody had big plans for the Twenty-ninth.

In late December, Norval was given six hours' notice to pack his bags and report again to the Twenty-ninth Division, which was taking part in a training exercise at Slapton Sands on the Channel coast. Although the troops did not know it, the unfolding invasion plan, Operation Overlord, called for the Twenty-ninth to storm the beach with the First Division on D-Day.

Norval was getting a taste of life on the battlefield—not just the ever-present danger of death or injury but also the dreary, filthy details. "Last night I had my first bath, using my helmet for a tub and only using one filling of water," he wrote after several days in the field. "I shave in the helmet when not wearing it. We brush our teeth using our canteen water sparingly. Mud, rock, sand & salt water are everywhere." It rained often during the exercises, making life generally miserable and basic hygiene difficult.

The troops also had to cope with the continual threat of German air raids. Although the training site was protected by barrage balloons, Norval dug a foxhole outside his tent in case he had to take cover on a moment's notice. Not far from the foxhole was another pit, one carved out not for protection but by an unexploded bomb that still lay buried within it. "It is well marked," he commented dryly.

From his position near the mock-assault beaches, he looked out on seas crowded with war vessels. To pass time, he focused his attention on a 33-foot-long navy

Norval observing the Twenty-ninth Division's
assault exercises at Land's End, January 1944.

ammunition ship used to carry torpedoes. "I would like
to get one after the war," he wrote. "We could build a
superstructure on it & make an excellent cabin cruiser
out of it."

The exercises were grueling and realistic, designed
to simulate the chaos and danger the troops would face
on D-Day, so that the noise, confusion, and shock of
battle would not be completely unfamiliar. Norval worked
with two other doctors and a staff of twelve enlisted
men trained in first aid. They spent their nights together
talking about medicine and sharing observations on the
training. He was "much happier away from the 110th,"
he told Fernie. "Kind of hate to go back." He even had
nice things to say about army meals, surely a sign of
contentment. "We . . . carry K rations, which contain

damned good food," he reported. Some soldiers might have disagreed.

Fernie must have grown even more anxious about her husband's safety as the buildup of Allied forces in England reached a climax. Why would he not want to go back to a safe unit behind the lines? Why would he be happier in the mud of combat training, observing not just rehearsals but also live shelling and real combat conditions on the beaches? Norval believed that he could be more useful in the field than in the hospital, in danger rather than in safety. He later wrote, "There is more 'medicine' & psychiatry to do here. One feels very close to these men and I want to do my best for them."

Although he was happier in the field, his letters continued to be filled with expressions of sadness and loneliness. The rain-soaked straw in his tent, he told Fernie, smelled sweetly reminiscent of her hair. He got his hands on some of the fabric used to make barrage balloons and sent it to her, suggesting it would make "excellent rain-coats" for Tom and me. And he never failed to look forward to the day when he could return home. "Please do a lot of praying that it will be all over soon & we can be together," he wrote. "Then we won't have to rely on memories." But for now something— duty and honor, perhaps, as well as an undeniable taste for adventure—called him to the battlefield.

In late January, he returned to the 110th Station Hospital, which was relocated to the Royal Victoria Hospital near Southampton. He continued to warn Fernie that he might be appointed division psychiatrist in a unit he could not name because of war censorship. The appointment would "mean a lot to me professionally and requires a higher rank than I now possess." Anticipating his wife's understandable anxiety, he tried to reassure her: "You needn't worry because there is no danger to it. My job will be to formulate plans and instruct medical officers in the Division as to the proper diagnosis, treatment & disposition of neuropsychiatric combat casualties."

Apparently she did not believe him. In a follow-up letter Norval wrote, affecting a jaunty tone, "You mentioned worrying about the things I am doing. No need of that, Sugar. Don't you realize that I lead a charmed life? You have me charmed & nothing can be done about that. I am your property, Fernie, being borrowed by the Army & this property is gonna return to you safe & sound." His underscoring of the phrase "return to you" reflected his optimism, but he was blunt about his preferred assignment: "I haven't heard about my possible transfer yet. I hope it happens." What Fernie did not know was that her husband was not merely hoping for a transfer to the Twenty-ninth Division; he was actively seeking one.

The Twenty-ninth Infantry Division dates back to America's hurried mobilization for World War I. It was created from a hodgepodge of National Guard units from Delaware, New Jersey, Maryland, Virginia, and the District of Columbia. After training for ten months, the Twenty-ninth participated in the Meuse-Argonne offensive in the latter days of the war to end all wars. Afterward, the Twenty-ninth returned home and resumed its original function as a National Guard unit. It was recalled to active service in the US Army in February 1941, almost a year before Pearl Harbor. The division, consisting of nearly 7,000 men and 656 officers, assembled at Fort Meade, Maryland, for its new duties.

The Twenty-ninth Division originally had four regiments, but one was transferred in March 1942, leaving three regiments organized roughly by geography: the 115th, made up of men mostly from Pennsylvania and Maryland; the 116th, with a large share of Virginians; and the 175th, composed of men from Baltimore. Each regiment was grouped in three battalions. When the Twenty-ninth was assigned to combat, several other units were attached to it, increasing the division's total strength to about 15,000 men.

Norval with members of the Twenty-ninth Division, to which he soon transferred, Land's End, January 1944.

After America declared war in December 1941, training intensified, and in the early fall of 1942 the soldiers of the Twenty-ninth boarded the two Queens—the *Queen Mary* and the *Queen Elizabeth*—for the journey to Scotland. The Twenty-ninth, part of the vanguard of Operation Bolero, was among the first divisions to arrive in the United Kingdom.

The division was first deployed to Tidworth Barracks, an old British army post about 10 miles from Stonehenge. The First Division, whose history would become intertwined with that of the Twenty-ninth, had trained at Tidworth before being shipped to the Mediterranean for the invasion of North Africa in November 1942. For a few months in late 1942, the Twenty-ninth was the only American division training in Britain.

By the time the Twenty-ninth arrived in England, the hour of peril for the British people had passed. The Royal Air Force had stubbornly denied Germany command of British skies, and Hitler had been forced to scrap Operation Sea Lion, the proposed cross-Channel invasion of Britain. Still, the island remained on alert, and the Twenty-ninth worked with British and Canadian forces to fortify local defenses. While they were at it, they helped harvest a crop of potatoes planted near the barracks by British soldiers now fighting in North Africa. For Christmas 1942, the men of the Twenty-ninth organized holiday parties for local children, who feasted on extra American rations. In the village of Adderbury a soldier dressed up as Saint Nick and handed out presents.

After a few months in England, the soldiers of the Twenty-ninth caught an unexpected glimpse of home when a Baltimore newspaper sent a newsreel to camp showing men of the 175th Regiment as they shipped out four months earlier. As Joseph Balkoski recounts in his history of the division, *Beyond the Beachhead,* "the newsreel showed such familiar Baltimore landmarks as Pimlico racetrack, Mount Vernon Square, and the Battle Monument. Soldiers from Baltimore roared and applauded as they recognized these scenes from home. But the room fell silent when the newsreel showed scenes of wives, sweethearts, parents, and children waving goodbye to their husbands, boyfriends, sons, and fathers. Some of the men glimpsed their loved ones, waving goodbye to them on camera."

As the Allied buildup continued, the Twenty-ninth was redeployed to the Devon-Cornwall peninsula in May. The 115th Regiment set up near the Bodmin-Launceston-Bake Manor area, the 116th around Plymouth, and the 175th near Penzance, Torquay, and Exeter. On the beaches and in the wastelands of nearby Dartmoor and Bodmin Moor, the men of the Twenty-ninth were put through hell in preparation for worse.

The wind-swept landscapes of Dartmoor, site of one of England's most notorious prisons, and Bodmin Moor seemed an unlikely training ground for men destined to fight on the farms and among the hedgerows of northern France. Men from the towns of Maryland and Virginia and the city streets of Baltimore found themselves knee deep in mud. They soon came to hate the moors, despite their bleak beauty, but no doubt emerged from the muck as better soldiers.

In his book *Twenty-nine, Let's Go!* Joseph Ewing, a veteran of the Twenty-ninth Division, described the moors as "broad stretches of barren terrain, utterly desolate, covered with thick, spongy grass, occasional shrubs, prickly evergreen and outcropping rock. It always seemed to be raining on the moors—a cold, stinging, horizontal rain, driven by the strong wind."

Norval had a different impression of the moors. He wrote to Fernie: "The magnificent beauty of Cornwall constantly reminds me of you. The moors have all the colors you love. The brilliant yellow of the gorse is like a certain summer dress you once wore. The gold of the bracken is like the flecks of your eyes. The breath-taking blue skies remind me of the aura of your presence. The soft rebound of the turf & peat-surfaced hills give the sensation of our bodies pressed close together. This is a beautiful country & you would love it."

The men trained seven days a week, and few were allowed furloughs. They subsisted on half-rations—a typical breakfast consisted of half an orange, a slice of bread, and a small portion of powdered eggs. Before they had a chance to enjoy these delicacies, they were expected to run 4 miles. Later in the day they picked their way through an obstacle course 2 or 3 miles long, and three times a week various units headed out of camp for a 30-mile march. This unusual intensity may have been an indication that the commanding officer, Maj. Gen. Leonard Gerow, lacked confidence in a division made up of so many National Guard units. Some of the career army officers—few, because the army was so small between the two world wars—believed that guardsmen lacked professional soldiers' discipline and focus and conducted their training accordingly.

The grind visibly wore down the men of the Twenty-ninth. When Gen. Charles Gerhardt took over the division in July 1943—Gerow was promoted to commander of the V Corps (the First and Twenty-ninth Divisions plus supporting units)—he immediately detected the low morale and granted the entire division three days off. He became a popular man.

Training became even more demanding in September 1943, and Norval's contact with the division increased. The men learned to handle a host of new weapons—including flamethrowers, bazookas, and bangalore torpedoes—intended to blast the Germans' concrete defenses and barbed-wire barriers in northern France. Soldiers of various units of the Twenty-ninth were deployed to Scotland to practice commando tactics. In the predawn blackness they rehearsed landings, bouncing in their landing crafts as other American soldiers fired live ammunition, including artillery, over their heads. When they landed and made their way across the sand, preplanted dynamite exploded to simulate conditions on the invasion beach.

A training operation known as Exercise Duck began in January 1944, and Norval traveled to Penzance and Land's End to observe the 175th Regiment. This training was tougher still. According to Balkoski, the exercise included live shelling of mock German defenses from offshore cruisers and destroyers as well as practice landings on beaches bristling with barbed wire and other obstacles.

By early 1944, a million American soldiers were training in Great Britain, preparing for the day that both friend and foe knew was imminent. In January the men of the Twenty-ninth received a visit from Gen. Bernard Montgomery, who had won a reputation for tactical brilliance in the sands of North Africa and was the overall commander of the invasion force's ground troops, subordinate only to the supreme commander, Gen. Dwight D. Eisenhower. Although not known for his warmth or humor, Monty prompted a laugh when he asked the soldiers of the 115th Regiment to remove their helmets while he talked to them. That way, they did not look quite so fearsome, he explained.

In letters to his wife, Norval continued to allude to a transfer, although he pretended that the decision was out of his hands. After a few days at a medical conference in mid-February and a stint during a court-martial, a task he did not enjoy, he reluctantly returned to the hospital. "How I have come to hate the unit," he said of the 110th, "which is in fact an excellent guarantee that I shall probably remain in it."

On February 28, 1944, Norval sent a birthday greeting to Fernie, who turned thirty-two on March 6.

> It's too bad we can't be together. . . . My present would be to tell you how sweet you are, how lovable and precious you are. I would like to look into your brown eyes and then kiss you. I want to smell your hair and hold you tightly. I want to whisper into your ear and tell you

that your birthday was a gift to me and our sons. You mean more to us three males than anything in the world, Fernie. I am so proud of you and happy that you are like you are. The boys will always be proud of such a wonderful mother and they will never cease to love and respect you.

You are more than a mother and a wife. You are a good companion; a lot of fun; a spiritual satisfaction; a joy and a sedative; an intellectual stimulus. My gift to you is to tell you that you are needed and appreciated by us more than anything or anybody in the world. If you experience a bit of satisfaction from this knowledge, . . . then I shall be happy. Because there is no gift in the world that means as much as how I feel about you, Fernie. My love for you is the most I have to contribute. . . .

Tell the boys how much I love their mother and themselves.

On March 14, 1944, Norval got the news for which he had been waiting, for which he had been preparing his wife: he was to be transferred to the Twenty-ninth Division.

He did not get the post he wanted, however. A superior had delayed Norval's paperwork, so the job of division psychiatrist went to someone else. Instead, he was assigned the position of battalion surgeon, the chief medical officer of a fighting unit of about nine hundred men. In this position he would supervise a second doctor and about forty medics and litter bearers at a station about half a mile behind the front lines. Once the aid station was set up, he would supervise recovery and rescue operations, emergency treatment of the wounded, and evacuation of the most severe cases to field hospitals or to England.

Despite Norval's assurances to Fernie, work as a battalion surgeon was more dangerous than serving as a division psychiatrist and infinitely more dangerous than serving in a station hospital far from the front. Although a battalion surgeon was not supposed to be in the vanguard, there was always the risk of artillery fire, snipers, or an enemy counterattack that might push through the front lines.

As Norval soon learned, the procedures and protocol for battlefield medicine were very specific. The medics were there to respond to wounded men, not to fight. Nevertheless, they endured the same punishing training as rank-and-file soldiers, except for weapons instruction; often there were no braver men on the battlefield. Steven Ambrose, in his book *Citizen Soldiers*, quotes Byron Whitmarsh of the Ninety-ninth Division: "There are worse things than being a rifleman in the infantry, not many, but being a medic is one of them. When the shelling and shooting gets heavy it is never long until there is a call for 'MEDIC!' That's when your regular GIs can press themselves to the bottom of their hole and don't need to go out on a mission of mercy."

Medics provided what first aid they could and administered morphine if the wounded soldier was conscious and in severe pain. They then helped or carried the wounded soldiers back to the aid station—often under enemy fire, despite their Red Cross armbands and internationally recognized status as noncombatants. The wounded were then handed over to doctors such as

Norval to administer dressings, plasma, antibiotics, and narcotics. If additional treatment was needed, the wounded were taken farther back to a clearing station and then transported by ambulance to a field or station hospital. The end of the line was the general hospital, located either in the United Kingdom or in the United States, where a higher level of treatment was available. When fighting was particularly intense, the aid stations functioned more as evacuation centers than as sites for anything more than the most rudimentary medical treatment.

Norval must have been delighted with his new work, although he tempered his enthusiasm when writing to Fernie. "Maybe I'll be a lot happier there," he wrote. "Most of the personnel of the 110th are in the dumps & quite brow beaten. . . . It is a pleasure (I hope) to get out of [the hospital service] into Army Ground Forces and thence into a field infantry unit. I believe I can do more for soldiers there than where I am now. Out of 15 months stay here in ETO [European Theater of Operations], I have done professional work for about only 6 or 7 of them."

Even though Norval did not get the job of division psychiatrist, his expertise in the field was becoming recognized within army medical circles. On March 10, just before his transfer became official, he gave a speech at a local meeting of British psychiatrists. The night before his speech, he and more than a dozen of his colleagues— "some of whom are well-known British brains," he told Fernie—settled into a bull session at a local inn. It was, he reported, "the best evening I have spent in England."

The following day he gave a talk on psychiatry in the army. He confessed that he was nervous—understandably, as he was not a formally trained psychiatrist and held only the junior officer rank of captain—but he was well received. He enjoyed the company of the British doctors. "They weren't like our psychiatrists at all—much more depth and humanity to them."

Responding to Fernie's concerns that he pack a gas mask, Norval continued to reassure her that even though he would soon face situations far more frightening than a room full of British psychiatrists, everything would work out fine. He also offered an insight into his politics in a discussion of the presidential race of 1944:

> What did you mean about remembering to carry my gas mask & be careful? Haven't I told you that I lead a charmed life & that you are the charm? Nothing is going to happen, Fernie. We have so much to do yet. Just keep the home fires burning, vote against socialized medicine, and don't change the furniture around too much.
>
> By the way, how are you going to vote if Roosevelt runs? I dislike him & his policy very much but I might vote for him if it would help win this war more quickly. What do you think? It may be possible that a change in administration would prolong (or delay) the war effort 6 months or so. . . . I would vote for John L. Lewis, Charlie Chaplin, or Al Capone if it would shorten this mess.

The coming of spring found Norval in the muck of Bodmin Moor. Although he and other staff officers were quartered in a manor house, he spent little time in those relatively luxurious surroundings. Mostly he was out in the moors, carrying heavy packs through the mud, sleeping outdoors, and otherwise preparing for the rigors to come. The troops were wet, dirty, and cold. "I have a wool-lined combat suit that is a big help but it is impossible to keep warm at night," he wrote. "No fires or lights allowed. No blankets. Just get under a bush, if there is one, & there usually isn't, and sleep fully clothed. I can't give you the location of the camp, but we are near the god-awful moors. Peat bogs are located on the top, sides, and bottoms of the mountains. Wild ponies run at the sight of a man." As daunting as this training might seem, he wrote his parents that he was "happier than at any other time in the army."

As busy as he was, my father allowed himself a certain amount of pathos as he learned of news from home. His medical partner and friend, Pete Hayman, was dying of a brain tumor, my brother and I were just getting over the measles, and his parents were selling their house to move into an apartment. "It seems that most of my boyhood was spent there," he told his wife. "It was a base from which to maneuver & make flank attacks on a bastion some 30 yards away, which was inhabited by a green-eyed, freckled-nose girl. Yes, it has meant a lot to me. . . . I hope too many things aren't changed when I get home. One cherishes a mental picture that resists change. A person hates to have his memories violated, because memories are one of our most prized possessions." In a letter to his parents, Norval described the old house as a "haven." "There I had & lost my first dog. It was the first place I brought my bride to. Everything centers there. Yes, I miss it all. The flowers, fruit, workshop, mint juleps, wine, sun-baths, learning photography, conversations, sickness, sunlight coming through the vines, the sweet nocturnal odor of petunias, all create in me a nostalgia that is overpowering. I could cry over it all. But that is life. Things must change."

Hundreds of thousands of American, British, and Canadian soldiers who made up the Allied Expeditionary Force—the assault force for D-Day—were toughening up for an invasion the likes of which even the most experienced veteran had never seen and could not imagine. For the Twenty-ninth Division, D-Day would be, quite literally, its baptism of fire.

For the First Division, the battle of France would be a continuation of their heroic and arduous service, which began in 1942 with the invasion of North Africa. Although nothing could compare with the enormity of D-Day, the troops of the First were no newcomers to combat. They had witnessed the horrors of war, had faced and beaten the German and Italian forces in North Africa, and had fought their way through Sicily. They had seen it all.

Not surprisingly, when the well-trained but green troops of the Twenty-ninth joined forces with the bat-tle-hardened First in early 1944, the result was a mili-tary culture clash. According to Balkoski's history, the First Division's troops were astonished to find that their brothers in the Twenty-ninth "actually wore their helmet straps hooked underneath their chins." No combat veteran worth his C rations would be caught wearing the goofy-looking chin straps—they were just a little too perfect, like wearing a starched collar to a baseball game. The veterans were casual about their headgear, buckling the straps in the back of the helmet. Just as surprising, the troops in Norval's division never grew stubble on their faces, no matter how tough training was, and always seemed to be washing their jeeps. Balkoski noted that the First Division, in the manner of all battle-weary combat veterans, found the Twenty-ninth's enthusiasm for training hilarious. During one joint exercise, they called out the unit's battle cry, "Twenty-nine, let's go." According to Balkoski, "One of the more sarcastic 1st Division old-timers put his hands to his mouth and yelled over, 'Go ahead, Twenty-nine, we'll be right behind you!'"

As D-Day grew nearer still, the Allied forces staged another full-dress rehearsal on the beaches of southwest England. These were gigantic affairs, designed not only to further toughen the troops but also to test how well the various forces, from infantry to engineers, worked together. The Twenty-ninth participated in these exercises on the beaches of Slapton Sands in early April, and Norval's medical unit rehearsed its routines while hundreds of soldiers played the role of casualties lined up in litters on the beach. Several weeks later, during a similar exercise on the same beach by the Fourth Division, German torpedo boats penetrated the training area and sank two large landing craft, killing more than 700 Americans. It was a warning of the havoc the

German navy might create in the English Channel if the Allied armada came under attack.

More than 200,000 additional American troops arrived in England in April, increasing the American presence to a million and a half servicemen. General Eisenhower described Great Britain as "the greatest operating military base of all time." Rural lanes were lined with piles of artillery shells; warplanes were towed through city streets, and, of course, men and women in uniform were everywhere. The English countryside was filled with American camps and American supply centers, protected from the peering eyes of enemy pilots but not necessarily a secret among local civilians. The Allied governments reminded civilians that they should watch what they said and to whom they said it. Secrecy was paramount. The Allies knew that their preparations were hardly a secret, but the date of the invasion and the invasion's landing target remained carefully guarded. The smallest piece of information—about troop movements, for example—might help the Germans deduce when the Allies were coming, and perhaps even where; advance warning of even two days could give the Germans an unbeatable advantage. Eisenhower advised the British to "draw a cordon round the British Isles, regulate all traffic from abroad, censor all communications."

Some information, however, was not so closely guarded. In fact, the Allies were deliberately careless with some of it. German intelligence had picked up a stream of communications from the First US Army Group, under the command of Gen. George Patton. The

Germans expected Patton to play a major role in the coming invasion, so they were not surprised to learn that he was in charge of a million-man force based in southeast England. It made sense: Southeast England faced the narrowest part of the English Channel, just a few miles across from the French city of Calais. It was the most likely site for an invasion.

Patton's army group, however, was an imaginary creation of Allied war planners. The transmissions were all fake; the tanks and landing craft left out in the open in southeast England were made of rubber. With any luck, when the Allies landed in Normandy the Germans would regard the movement as a diversion to distract them from Patton's anticipated landing at Calais.

In mid-May, General Eisenhower set the date for the invasion: June 5.

The life of an American soldier training for D-Day was not "as easy as is depicted in Life Magazine." After a little more than a month with the Twenty-ninth Division, Norval was able to scale rope landing nets, run 100 yards with a man on his back, march 4 miles in thirty-five minutes, chart and follow a compass course, and do thirty-four pushups. "I no longer have a pot-belly, and I can hike 25 miles without too much dis-comfort," he reported on April 23.

Norval was popular with the men, particularly because he had volunteered for a combat unit. He got to know many of them when he was given the job of reading and censoring outgoing mail. Decades later, several veterans of the Twenty-ninth Division shared

Norval digging a foxhole during training exercise on
Bodmin Moor, May 1944. This is one of the last known
photographs of him.

their memories with me. One of them was B.R. Eastridge,
a second lieutenant at the 115th's regimental headquarters in Bodmin, in Cornwall, who had heard my father
give a lecture at headquarters about the psychological
problems of combat soldiers. To illustrate his point to
what may have been a skeptical audience, my father compared soldiers in combat to metal under stress; if the
metal is bent continuously, eventually it will break. Even
well-trained soldiers have their breaking points, he told
his audience.

Eastridge sought out my father during a field exercise to talk more about combat fatigue. Perhaps my

father's advice helped him, for Eastridge later told me that he was one of only four company officers in the 115th who lasted the 337 days and nights from D-Day to VE Day.

Other soldiers described my father as a tough taskmaster when it came to military hygiene. If he spotted a soldier spitting, he barked, "Soldier, swallow that!" One veteran remembered that Norval "inspected our barracks with white gloves after clean-up, always finding dirt but always being very nice about it." In fact, he was so adamant about keeping the barracks clean that some of his men nicknamed him "Dusty" Carter.

Chester Adams, a medic, recalled that my father spent a lot of time with the men who lined up daily at sick call, some of whom may not have been physically ill. As the invasion date approached, veterans told me, some soldiers were suddenly bothered by old football injuries and other conditions. Norval did not dismiss these men or their complaints. "They have something on their minds, and I want to talk to them," he told Adams.

My father led by example, training hard with the men under his command. During training on the moors he had a close call when he sank into a bog, but a corporal quickly pulled him to safety using his rifle. He was also making a name for himself as a marksman, although he would not be carrying a weapon into battle. He qualified as an expert in the .45 caliber Colt automatic pistol, hitting every one of a series of bobbing targets—perhaps the payoff for his youthful habit of shooting at road signs.

A sure sign that he would soon be in combat came when Norval was told to pack up his personal effects and ship them home to his wife. If, for all his bravado and assurances, he did not make it home, somebody should know his wishes, he wrote to his parents in a letter dated May 4:

> It looks like we have a very dangerous job ahead of us, and the men & officers are exceptionally well trained. The infantryman today is quite a diversified soldier and he is (as you know he always was) the backbone of the Army. I am proud to be able to help them out & ease things for them. But I'll have to admit that I am a bit afraid of the future. Hell is apt to break loose. Shellfire & bombing will be terrific. I pray that even though we are afraid, we can carry on bravely & courageously. I am very concerned about Fernie—'cause I know she worries about me & I hate that more than anything else. I love her & the boys more than I can ever tell & I hate to think & really can't believe that I may not get back. Be sure that she gets along all right & treat her as you always have in the past. She is the best thing in the world. Thank heavens my insurance is paid up and that will always take care of her & the boys.
>
> Another thing: If I don't come back, Fernie may want to marry again someday. It will be best if she does, and Mom, and Dad, please don't ever criticize her for it. It would be the best thing for her & my sons. And I would be happy to know that. I'll never mention this again in future letters because it hurts me inside to do so, but please remember what I have said.

In mid-May Norval moved from the moors to one of the Twenty-ninth Division's staging encampments near Plymouth. Throughout southern England, training and rehearsals came to an end as the assault troops moved to camps closer to the ports. Troops marched through towns, and long convoys of tanks and trucks snaked though the countryside—amazingly, all undetected by the enemy.

Once the troops were in the assembly camps, supplies were handed out, food was plentiful—and anxiety was overwhelming. During the preceding weeks and months, the troops at least had training to take their minds off the future. Now, as they assembled in camps to await embarkation, they were idle.

Before being moved to his assembly area, Norval managed to snag a twenty-four-hour pass and spent the day in a nearby fishing village. Just after ordering a lobster lunch he received word to report back to his unit immediately. "No rest for the weary," he wrote. That night, on May 13, 1944—my fourth birthday—he took a final look at the letters from his wife and parents and friends. What comfort they had given him during his desolate nights; he often remarked, as so many other soldiers have, that letters from home drove away the loneliness, at least for a while, and brought a smile to his face. He could not keep them any longer. "Tonight I am doing something I hate to do," he told her. "It is necessary to destroy all my letters from you & my friends. It hurts, but, Fernie, hell, I love you so much."

The isolation of the staging areas was not yet complete, so he could still write home. On May 15, a few days after learning that Pete Hayman, his friend and medical partner, had died, leaving a wife and three young children, he wrote to John Morris and shared his secret:

> I have been transferred to a battalion which is part of a Combat Team and I am its surgeon. It is interesting work but rough as hell and I'll admit I fear for the future. However, I am happier here than anywhere else in the Army. A swell bunch of officers & men who are exceptionally well trained. I don't suppose I have ever had a chance to be brave in life & to act with courage but it looks as though the opportunity will present itself. I don't fear death per se, but it really depresses me to think I may never see Fernie, Tom, & W.F. again. . . . I'll never tell Fernie, but I requested the transfer. It is impossible to say why, my feelings & emotions are all mixed up about it, but I was unhappy in the Station Hospital & I am happy here—or as much so as one could be away from home.

To relieve the boredom and stress of the waiting period, the Allied commanders allowed the troops to loosen up a bit. The Twenty-ninth's divisional band played for the troops on May 19, and Norval lay in the sun, which was making one of its infrequent appearances that month, and soaked in the music—some Sousa, Victor Herbert, and popular tunes. "It was really good . . . reminded me of my clarinet days," he wrote.

Food was everywhere, and he was tickled that tobacco and candy were free. "We don't have to buy it now," he exulted. "Night before last we were given a Hershey bar (nuts) apiece. Everyone nearly went wild over the stuff. It was the first milk chocolate I have had since Xmas & many men haven't had any since

August, '42!" In addition to chocolate, the men were given condoms, although not for the customary purpose—they were just the right size to slip over watches and cigarettes to keep them dry. "It is somewhat amusing to see a man pull out big packages of [cigarettes] covered with a condom, or see it around his wrist," he wrote.

To keep his men in shape and relieve the monotony, Norval had them play touch football and volleyball. He conducted long drills with his outfit's litter bearers to keep their hands tough and well calloused. He reported that he was "better physically than ever in my life."

In late May, the staging areas were locked tighter and the men were prohibited from entering or leaving; visitors had already been banned. Barbed wire separated the assault troops from the armed guards on the outside. Before camp was sealed and mail discontinued, Norval sent Fernie what he knew would be his last letter for weeks. In it he shared the memories he held close as he prepared for battle, memories of his wife when they were sweethearts and of the music they loved:

> The dark red wool dress you wore one winter with some kind of pin at the neck. . . . One Sunday winter afternoon when we had the house to ourselves—your mother & Bess were away, & we played the piano & clarinet, then the phonograph, & kissing each other every few minutes. My, how I loved you! You were on my mind all the time then & I was so impatient for the day to arrive when we could marry. You were something to have. Now I think of you, loving you, and long

for the day when we can be together again. That day, we can spend by playing over those old records, Fernie, and & telling Tom & W.F. how much they mean to us.

What did W.F. do on his birthday? Did he make a wish & blow out all his candles? What was the wish? . . . What have you planned for Tom this summer? I would like for him to learn something about plant & animal cells and something of the principles of magnification. These things would give him an idea of structure, unity, and basic design of things. . . .

You should see my underwear. I wear some long woolens & also the pull-over sweater under my shirt. They haven't been washed for 2 weeks now. The more unwashed they are the more water-repellent they become. And not only water-repellent!

Remember, Fernie, that I love you and Tom and Walter Ford more than anything in the world. I always have & always shall be true to you all, and I hope to be able to conduct myself like a gentleman should during the next few weeks or months.

Leaving her with that image of a soldier's life, he said that letters would be few in the coming weeks.

In fact, the invasion was just days away.

In their enclosed camps the men of the Twenty-ninth and the other assault divisions were learning what fate—or rather General Eisenhower and his aides—had in mind for them beginning June 5. The Twenty-ninth was to team with the First Division to attack a Normandy beach code-named Omaha. The 116th Regiment would hit the beach at H-Hour, 6:30 a.m. Norval's 115th Regiment would follow in the afternoon, unless the 116th ran into trouble and the 115th was needed earlier. On D-Day the two regiments would technically be under the command of the First Division. The following day, when the Twenty-ninth's commander landed, the division would return to its familiar command structure.

The officers had models of the invasion beaches with fairly precise locations of enemy defenses, right down to machine-gun emplacements. Omaha Beach promised to be the most difficult of the five invasion points—above the crescent-shaped beach rose a high bluff that made for a perfect defensive position. It also was the most critical: If the assault was pushed into the sea, the American Fourth Infantry Division, which was to land on Utah Beach, to the west of Omaha, would be cut off from the British and Canadian beaches—code-named Gold, Sword, and Juno—to the east.

The invasion of France could be won or lost on Omaha Beach.

The troops studied the mountain of intelligence the Allies had accumulated, and they were given life belts and anti-seasickness pills—a wasted effort for many, as it turned out—along with grenades and ammunition. During these last days in camp Norval examined a soldier named E.J. Hamill, from the First Battalion of the 115th Regiment, who had come down with a virus. My father ordered him to the dispensary. On a visit later, Norval told Hamill that he was too ill to make the trip; he could land later, with the subsequent waves of troops. Crestfallen, Hamill begged to be allowed to rejoin his buddies in the 115th for their appointment on

Omaha Beach. Norval was having none of it and started to walk away, but then he stopped, turned to Hamill, and said: "If you are determined to go, I will release you." He reminded him that they would be on the same landing craft. "I'll be ready to help if you need me," he told the soldier. Hamill rejoined his unit.

At seven o'clock in the morning on May 31, Norval boarded an LCVP (landing craft, vehicle/personnel). He had risen at four to eat breakfast and observe several soldiers who had developed what he called "mild panic states." They were easily dealt with, he wrote, but another soldier in Company D had developed an uncontrollable obsession. He probably should have been sent to the rear, but Norval thought the soldier's sudden departure would have a bad effect on his buddies. "I'll keep him until we make the far shore" he wrote in his journal. "Then if he can't adjust to battle, it will be easier to send him back to a hospital."

The LCVP took them along the River Tamar to another vessel, an LCI(L) (landing craft infantry, large), which transported them to Plymouth Harbor. In the harbor, hundreds of vessels assembled and waited for orders to begin the 100-mile crossing to Normandy. The weather was fine that day, sunny and a bit cool, Norval noted. It would not stay that way for long.

The next day, as the landing craft sailed out of Plymouth Harbor and headed eastward for Portland Harbor in Dorset, he handed out antinausea medication. Sitting out on the gun deck, he wrote: "You seem so near, Fernie. The day is perfect for dreaming. Sun is brite, clouds are billowy, and the water has 5-foot swells of blue, green, and purple. Some white caps present. The ship rolls and pitches lazily. We spotted a shark off starboard but it hastily left."

As land disappeared, Norval looked out toward the vast expanse of sea on the starboard side. Over the horizon was France. Under the seas might be German E boats. In the skies might be the German air force. He noted that he was wearing a helmet and an inflated life belt—just in case. After safely sailing into Portland Harbor, he puzzled, "I just can't understand why Jerry doesn't come over!" It was amazing, indeed: an assault force of 5,000 ships and 150,000 men on the move and not an enemy airplane or vessel to be found. Later that night he made a quart of homemade "gin" out of juniper oil, glycerin, and alcohol mixed with some lemon crystals and water, and he and a few other officers had a Tom Collins. The men agreed it was nice to have a doctor on board. "Each of us had only a short drink," he wrote. "We all wanted to feel tops for D-Day." The unit proceeded along the coast, heading for its point of embarkation. On June 2, another fine day, their landing craft sailed into Weymouth Harbor, west of the Isle of Wight, where they waited for the order to cross the Channel.

For the thousands of soldiers aboard the vessels, the waiting was becoming intolerable. For Norval, however, it brought a little adventure. While in Weymouth Harbor, he got permission to take a rubber raft to another landing craft to get some medical supplies. The winds were beginning to pick up, churning up the sea and making the short journey more difficult that it ought to have been. He wrote:

> This afternoon, after much red tape, I was permitted to take a rubber Good-Year life raft and go after my salve. It is supposed to hold 6 men but 3 sailors and myself fully loaded it. Tom, you and W.F. would have enjoyed that trip of 300 yards. The water is rough and quite a breeze blowing. It was difficult to get in the thing. It bobbed and weaved like a feather in a whirlwind. I wanted the fun of going in first, and luckily I dropped in without falling in the drink. It was difficult to paddle and navigate because of its light weight, no draw of any depth and because the wind blew us about. Finally we arrived at LCLI #413 and got aboard. . . . Stayed long enough to kid and be kidded, chewed the fat a bit, listened to some stilted and awkward jokes about not seeing one another again until we hit shore in France. Departed with an awkward feeling, knowing that I would not see some of these splendid chaps again.

After returning from his visit, Norval broke the tension in his landing craft by teasing some of his fellow officers, particularly the one in charge of supplying food. "I told them that instead of the K and C rations that we're eating we should be having a lot of steak, canned ham and chicken, and other delicacies," he wrote. "I really laid it on. All the other craft had those things, I lied, and they all swallowed the bait and fell to vigorous discussion. They want to send me ashore to finagle such a thing from [the quartermaster] but security forbids such a thing at this time. No one can go ashore. Even the skipper went in under guard. Well, it was fun anyway. I didn't think they would bite, because I fooled them twice before. A few days ago I made them believe that we were going to be fed water-melon on our last day in marshaling area and that we wouldn't leave until then. Of course, Fernie, this fruit is non-existent in England. But some of them were surprised when we left without it. By the way, what does a banana taste like? I have forgotten. I saw a 50-cent piece today (USA) and I couldn't remember whether it was a quarter or a half-dollar. Can you beat that? I just don't think in terms of dollars and cents now."

The rations were starting to run low, an indication that the invasion could be only hours away. The mood in the landing craft turned somber. Norval attended briefings where everybody was "dead serious. Faces immobile and deeply lined. Young men look old. No fear shown, no nervous finger-tapping, just quiet, deeply thoughtful immobility. . . . To bed with minds too heavy for thinking. Everyone sleeps, but restlessly."

He waterproofed everything he would be carrying to the beach, including a camera. That item was "taboo, but I must have a picture of the thing that is so vital to me. I intend to sneak up onto the bridge when we make our approach and get a few snaps."

The assistant commander of the Twenty-ninth Division, Brig. Gen. Norman Cota, brought together some of the unit's top commanders for a final briefing and pep talk. A veteran of the North Africa invasion, he did not spare his men any of the realities he had experienced. Cota predicted that there would be mass confusion on the beaches. "The landing craft aren't going in on schedule, and people are going to be landed in the wrong place," he said. "Some won't be landed at all. The enemy will try, and have some success, in preventing our gaining 'lodgement.' But we must improvise, carry on, not lose our head."

On Sunday June 4 the men in Norval's landing craft practiced loading their rubber life rafts. Religious services on board the vessel were packed. He wrote his last journal entry before hitting the beach:

> Most of us have a strong spiritual feeling about this affair. We realize we are up against a well trained, well equipped and a well disciplined enemy who will resist and counter-attack with great zeal. But we realize we are fighting for a way of living that is fundamentally right in the eyes of God and man, and the ideals of the enemy are wrong. Therefore we are not fighting for our own hides but for you folks back home and for people everywhere. I look about the deck at the men. It is a terrible thing to know that in 24 hours some are not going to even be able to enjoy what we intend to win. All of us think of home, our wives, children, and parents, and hope that we can see them again.
>
> Fernie, my sweetheart, I feel that I shall see you again. You and the boys. But if I don't, I want you to remember that my love for you cannot be said or put on paper. It can only be felt. You have meant every-

thing to me that is good and happy. Since tomorrow is D-Day (and we weigh anchor tonight), I won't be able to write for a few days. May God help us in our mission. I hope to return to you all. God bless you Fernie, you Tom, and you Walter Ford.

On the night of June 5, after a day's postponement because of bad weather, the greatest invasion force ever assembled in the history of the world sailed from southern England.

Sacrifice

6 In the darkness off the coast of Britain, where four years earlier soldiers had watched for signs of Hitler's invasion fleet, thousands of ships sailed from their points of embarkation into the English Channel. The minesweepers, battleships, cruisers, destroyers, landing craft, and other support vessels maneuvered to take their assigned positions in the battle order and then set out for France.

But the assault troops would not be the first Allied soldiers in France on this day. Operation Overlord was already under way.

Just after midnight, paratroopers and glider-borne troops had landed behind the beaches to destroy some of

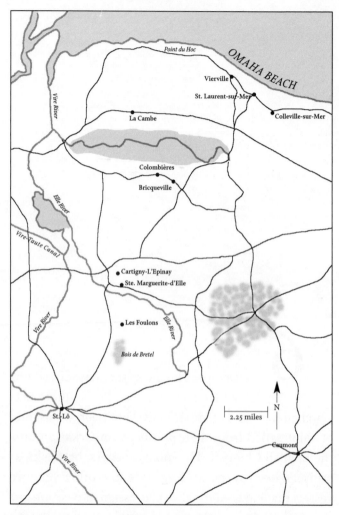

Map of Northern France showing the towns along the Twenty-ninth Division's path from Omaha Beach to St.-Lô.

the enemy's communications and defenses, sow confusion, and secure bridges and other vital positions. From their assault vessels in the Channel, the soldiers heading for Normandy heard the rumble of bombers en route to France, where they would blast away at Fortress Europe.

Miles away to the east, where the Channel narrows between Dover and Calais, the nonexistent First Army Group also was on its way to France. The armada consisted of motor launches carrying balloons to deceive German radar. German operators were convinced that their screens showed the approach of the main invasion force, headed for Calais, where Hitler expected the Allied attack. As a result, senior German commanders held back their panzer reserves for critical hours on D-Day, uncertain whether the Normandy landing was the main Allied effort.

Just before six o'clock, as the cover of night yielded grudgingly to an overcast morning, the Allied warships in the Channel opened fire on the five invasion beaches scattered along a 50-mile stretch of French coastline. From their landing craft, heading toward the shore, the assault troops watched in awe as Normandy exploded before their eyes. Ernest Hemingway, bound for Omaha Beach in his role as a war correspondent, watched as the USS *Texas* fired on the German position: "Those of our troops who were not wax grey with seasickness, fighting it off, trying to hold onto themselves before they had to grab for the steel side of the boat, were watching the *Texas* with looks of surprise and happiness. There would be a flash like a blast furnace from the 14-inch guns of the *Texas*. . . . Then the yellow brown smoke would cloud out and, with the smoke still rolling, the concussion and the report would hit us, jarring men's helmets." Hemingway heard a GI exclaim, "Look what they're doing to those Germans. I guess there won't be a man alive there."

It was an illusion, as the troops soon learned. The Germans, under Field Marshal Erwin Rommel, had spent many months fortifying the beachfront defenses. The Allied naval bombardment did not deter the defenders, especially those on the bluffs above Omaha Beach, and the air bombardment, hampered because of cloud cover, fell uselessly behind the German front lines.

The 116th Regiment, temporarily under the command of the First Division, was to attack the westernmost sectors of Omaha Beach. The battle plan called for Norval's unit, the 115th Regiment, to come ashore later, when the beach would be secure and the men of the Twenty-ninth Infantry Division would be pushing inland beyond the village of St. Laurent-sur-Mer.

But, as Gen. Norman Cota had predicted to the officers of the Twenty-ninth, little went according to plan that terrible morning on Omaha Beach. The story of the bloodshed and valor of those long hours has been chronicled in many books and films and has found a lasting and deserving place in the nation's collective memory. The enemy's fire was accurate and devastating. Landing craft were blown out of the water, men were cut down before reaching the beach, bodies lay sprawled on the sand or floated in the tide. Omaha was a killing ground. Although the Allies made good progress at the other invasion beaches, on Omaha forward movement stalled until, with courage and determination, the GIs carved out a small beachhead, ensuring the operation's success.

The story of how the first wave regrouped after the initial shock of landing is for others to tell. Here, it is important to add only that when the men of the 116th Regiment became bogged down on the beach, the schedule for the second wave was moved up. Instead of landing in the afternoon, my father and the rest of the 115th Regiment were ordered to shore before noon.

E.J. Hamill, the enlisted man whom Norval had visited in the dispensary in England and cleared for the landing, stood with him as their craft approached the coast. When a voice over the loudspeaker told them that they would have to fight their way inland, they were aghast. According to the plan, now in tatters, the beach should have been secured and resistance overcome by the time their unit arrived. Instead, the 115th Regiment was heading toward chaos.

The landing craft was one of twelve transporting the 115th Regiment to the beaches, now partially obscured by smoke and pockmarked by shells. The landing craft generally seen in the films of amphibious landings were transported across the Channel by a mother ship, making only the final leg, between the transport and the beach, on their own. The vessels transporting Norval's regiment were a good deal larger, and his own craft, an LCI (number 554), was large enough to make the journey across the Channel on its own and shallow enough to land directly on the beach. It held more than 200 troops, weighed nearly 250 tons, and had a pair of landing ramps to disgorge its cargo on the beach.

The craft's size made navigation through the enemy's tidal obstacles tricky. The obstacles, many of which were mined, were supposed to have been removed by the time the 115th Regiment approached the beach, but like so many other parts of the invasion plan, this assignment could not be accomplished on schedule because of heavy enemy fire. The captain in charge of the vessels quickly realized that he could not land his men on the designated sector of the beach. Opposition was too fierce, and the beach was congested with pinned-down troops and the remains of disabled landing craft, tanks, and trucks.

On the port side, to the east of the original landing position, the Eighteenth Regiment of the First Division was beginning to move inland. The landing craft carrying the 115th Regiment were ordered to change course and land behind the Eighteenth in a sector a mile to the east, code-named Easy Red. As Norval, Hamill, and their fellow soldiers braced themselves for the moment when the landing ramp descended, the air above them was filled with German lead. Bullets pinged off the sides of the landing craft. Shells landed nearby, creating geysers of seawater. One of the landing craft hit an obstacle; another broke a rudder. At about eleven o'clock, the ramps were lowered, and the First Battalion lunged out into neck-high water.

Compared with the carnage on other sectors of Omaha, resistance on Easy Red was light by the time they landed. The American naval bombardment had caused fires in the tall marsh grass between the beach and the bluffs, and the smoke helped screen the landings as the morning wore on. But the beach was filled with evidence of the bloody struggle of the past few hours. Other landing craft floated listlessly, abandoned or damaged during the earlier landings. The dead and the wounded lay everywhere.

Norval's unit made it to the beach and quickly crossed it, despite German small-arms fire and artillery. Casualties were light, but my father had work to do once he had made his way toward a bluff that rose from the shore. Although he had treated the wounds that war could inflict, both in the hospital and in training in England, what was new was the pressure of working under enemy fire.

He and Chester Adams, a litter bearer, moved carefully among the wounded. As Norval treated the men, Adams held their hands. Some of the wounds were horrifying, and Norval sensed that Adams was becoming distracted by the gruesome sight of so many casualties. "Chessie," he said gently, "don't look at all that. Keep your eyes right here."

The slopes beyond the beach were sown with mines, and although paths had been cleared, the troops moved slowly and with great care. The First Battalion advanced about a mile inland and dug in for the night. But a burst of mortar fire during the night severely wounded the battalion's commander, Lt. Col. Richard Blatt. Norval raced to the colonel's side, treated him, and helped carry him back to the beach for evacuation.

The colonel's head wound was fatal, however, and he died after being evacuated to England.

For the men of the 115th Regiment, D-Day had not been nearly as terrible as it had for their comrades in the 116th Regiment or in the lead units of the First Infantry. By nightfall the Omaha beachhead was secured, but tenuously—the Americans had moved only about a mile inland. The cost of that small piece of France had been high: nearly 5,000 casualties, according to Joseph Balkoski.

Field Marshal Rommel, who on D-Day was in Germany for his wife's birthday, had always contended that an Allied invasion had to be met with an immediate counterattack. The invasion had to be stopped at the beach and thrown back into the sea. If the Allies secured a beachhead, he believed, the battle was lost. His superior, Field Marshal Gerd von Rundstedt, commander of the German armies in Western Europe, maintained that a counterattack launched later could still be effective if the Allies were heavily dependent on seaborne reinforcements. Rommel may have been right. If the panzers at Calais had been released immediately and a few other factors had played out differently, the invasion might have been repulsed.

During the afternoon of June 6, the 115th Regiment moved toward the village of St. Laurent-sur-Mer. Norval's First Battalion did meet a counterattack and nearly ran out of ammunition before reinforcements and stragglers helped beat back the assault. They took a position south of the village while the Second and Third Battalions probed and then took the village late that day and early the next morning. As the First Battalion moved through the outskirts of St. Laurent on June 7, its troops saw French civilians for the first time. "The French here in Normandy haven't been as badly treated by the Germans as the newspapers led me to believe," Norval later wrote.

Once Norval's division moved farther inland, the men found themselves on terrain very different from the open, rolling moors of southwest England, where they had trained so hard for so long. In Normandy, as in England, hedgerows lined the countryside, separating one farmer's fields from another. English hedgerows were thin borders of small trees and bushes; Norman hedgerows, some of which were 2,000 years old, could be 6 feet tall or more and 10 feet wide at their base. Composed of earth, stone, vines, and small trees with deep, tangled roots, they formed a maze that obscured visibility and allowed for extremely effective defensive positions. Allied planners, concerned chiefly with getting the troops off the beach, had not adequately considered the conditions inland. The hedgerows caught the well-trained Allied soldiers by surprise.

To the shaken and confused men of the First Battalion, Norval was a familiar sight, frequently exposing himself to enemy fire as he tended to the wounded. Donald Null, a soldier assigned to the battalion's heavy-weapons company, remembered, "Carter was very visible . . . always out in the field with the wounded when we had battles, giving shots and I-Vs." Other officers later recalled that Norval often was too close, in their judgment, to the fighting. In the terrible calculations of combat, battalion surgeons were considered vital—too important to lose to a sniper or a grenade.

As his unit moved forward, he had at least two close calls. In one instance, as he and a sergeant were traveling in a jeep, a mortar landed nearby. In what he described as "a near-hit," they were blown off the road. On another of his forays to the front, a sniper's bullet nicked him in the leg.

Norval shook off these brushes with death. As a responsible officer and a doctor with psychiatric training, he undoubtedly understood that many men, particularly the medics, were looking to him for leadership, and he chose to lead by example. Capt. John Ryan, the commanding officer of A Company, later remembered that Norval "was up there getting his medics organized and on the job, and literally was able to pick up our wounded as they became casualties." Ryan himself became a casualty, although not as a result of enemy fire. He was bitten on the hip by an insect, probably a spider, and the wound became so infected that he was sent to Norval's aid station just behind the lines. He later noted that Norval "was always there to help the men in any way he could. Somehow he managed to get a few little extras to offer the men in addition to medical expertise—coffee, juice, milk, things that were in short supply—and had these items on hand to console those he found needed his care." He even managed to secure Ryan a fresh pair of long johns when Ryan's infection broke and soiled his clothes.

They happened to be together when the first mail arrived for the troops since the invasion had begun.

Fernie had sent photographs of Tom and me, and Norval showed them to Ryan. My father admitted to Ryan how much he missed us and wanted to be with us.

They also must have spoken about the psychological effects of combat, because when one of Ryan's officers became, in Ryan's words, "a little shaky as a result of his combat experience," he brought him to see Norval. As Ryan related the encounter, Norval "just put his arm around his shoulder and said he would take care of him. He treated the man, rested him up, and in a few days returned him to duty in our company."

In a related incident, my father found George Schultz, one of the medics, cowering behind a hedgerow, paralyzed with fear, when he should have been tending to casualties. Norval, who for nearly two years had studied the effect of fear on soldiers' psyches, put his observations into practice. He did not yell or shout but said simply, "Come on with me. Let's go out there and get them." Schultz would remember that my father's firm but gentle nudge snapped him out of his fears.

That kind of leadership helped Norval's subordinates not only in the medical unit but also among combat troops on the front lines. The commander of the First Battalion's Company C, Capt. William Kenney, recalled that "to those of us in the infantry, it was an incentive to push forward under any situation, because we knew the medics were right there with us and would render assistance at all times, led of course by Cap'n Carter."

By Friday, June 9, the First Battalion was slogging its way through flooded marshlands toward the village of Colombières, which had been raided by another

American unit the night before. Norval and his assistant, Lt. Roger E. Watson, were on their way through the village in a jeep when a French civilian stopped them and asked them to help his injured children. According to Wyatt Blassingame in his book *Medical Corps Heroes in World War II*, they never hesitated: "Go with him, Roger," Norval said. "I'll move on with the outfit. You can catch up with us." While Watson was tending to the children, a group of German soldiers surrounded him. Ignoring them, Watson continued with his work, and the Germans eventually left. Watson later received the Silver Star for his bravery, very likely on my father's recommendation.

As the 115th Regiment moved from Colombières toward Bricqueville, a mortar shell landed near Billy Melander of Tonawanda, New York, near Buffalo. Billy was thrown against a wall; shrapnel was embedded in his leg, and he had cuts on his forehead and chin. He was brought back to the aid station, where Norval removed the shrapnel and stitched him up. "You look too young to be at the front," he told Melander, and then promised him that he would be okay. Shortly afterward, a rumor swept the aid station that a German counterattack was on the verge of breaking through and the post might soon be surrounded by enemy forces. The sound of artillery and small-arms fire close by seemed to confirm the rumors, and the staff and the injured who could walk were about to flee to the rear. Summoned to the battalion command post, Norval was ordered to round up volunteers to move forward and get the wounded back to the aid station.

Melander was among those who volunteered to serve as a litter bearer.

The aid station was soon inundated with casualties. Decades later, Melander recalled his amazement at how skillfully Norval and his associates treated the many wounded and prepared the worst cases for evacuation. "Even today, some fifty years later, as I shave and look into the mirror, I see those faint scars on my forehead and chin and thank God that Captain Carter was there to tend to me in my hour of need," he told me.

On Sunday morning, June 11, as the beachhead was expanded and reinforcements came pouring in to Normandy, Norval and some other officers left the First Battalion's position, near L'Epinay-Tesson, in search of a facility to serve as an evacuation hospital. Near the village of Cartigny-L'Epinay they found a chateau owned by René Pagny, a limestone quarrier. The site was perfect: To the west was an open field suitable for a large number of hospital tents; to the east was another open space large enough to serve as an airstrip to evacuate the wounded to England.

Norval and three other officers approached the chateau in their jeep just before noon. The owner's daughter, Odette Pagny, a woman in her midforties, was thrilled to see them, as I later learned from letters she wrote to my mother. "There are the Americans, father," she exclaimed. "Look at the star on their car." Approaching Norval, Odette said, "God bless you. My home is yours." He shook Odette's hand. Just two hours earlier, German troops had been in the chateau. Now, after four years of suffering under Nazi occupation, the

Odette Pagny and her family's chateau, where Norval and the Twenty-Ninth Division set up an evacuation hospital.

day of liberation finally had arrived. For Odette, my father was the face and symbol of the liberators.

They set up a medical base in the chateau, and over the next few days Odette prepared meals for them, not failing to notice that these busy men never sat down while they ate. Odette looked up to them not only as her liberators but also as her personal protectors. "He was so kind, and we were so much in danger," she told my mother. "The battle in night over air and ground was terrible. I was so afraid . . . I was always with them. Nobody could tell you and describe what he was, only us who were with them know. . . . What a gentleman he was." She dreaded the day they would have to move on, leaving her unprotected. At night she slept near their room while planes flew overhead and the sound of explosions and small-arms fire riddled the night.

Just after midnight on June 12, word passed through the line that the First Battalion would attack enemy positions over the Elle River—actually little more than a creek—and beyond the village of Ste. Marguerite-d'Elle. The troops moved out at 3:30 a.m. After marching a mile and a half, they halted while the battalion opened an artillery barrage against the German position that lasted half an hour. The Americans, coming down the exposed slope on the north side of the creek, attempted to cross the Elle, but the German defenders, dug in on the high ground on the south side, were in an excellent position to fire on the Americans. They let loose with deadly machine-gun and mortar fire, pinning down the First Battalion for hours. The unit suffered 100 casualties, and the Third Battalion, which was operating nearby, suffered 130. Medics moved forward and brought many of the wounded to the aid station; ambulances or jeeps took the worst cases to the chateau where Norval was based. Odette watched as he and his men worked tirelessly on the mangled soldiers, some who would survive and some who would not.

On June 12 the First Battalion pulled back and was given forty-eight hours of rest. In his first letter to his wife written from Normandy, Norval wrote:

This is the first day we have been permitted to write, and it certainly is a privilege. It lessens the lonesomeness to be able to tell you I miss you and I love you. I have been in France since June 6 and have been in some tough actions. I ache for home and you and the boys—the present circumstances make the ache even more acute. Life is now very precious and dear, and home is what life means to me.

The morale of the men in my battalion is high even though the losses of officers & men have been heavy. We are very tired physically and mentally. Sleep is a rare elixir. Hot meals are non-existent. A bed is a memory. I haven't had my shoes off my feet but once in 10 days. We have been under heavy fire but are giving more than we receive—in other words we are winning. I have lost some valuable aid men and have recommended citations for quite a few others. All my men have done a grand job—a super human job. My health is good (except my nerves) except for a mild conjunctivitis. A gnat got in my eye! Imagine!

Tell Tom & W.F. I still think of them. Also tell them they are very fortunate to be living in America. All people, English, French, and German, envy the USA. The people of France have welcomed us in a way that is heart-breaking—the Germans in a way that is heart-stopping. The latter are excellent soldiers and superbly equipped. They fight tenaciously & give ground at great cost to us. We are only overwhelming them with masses of manpower and materiel. We shall probably be sent to a rest area soon—we need it. . . . Some of my best friends are no more.

I love you, Fernie, and think of you each day. Pray that we shall soon be together again.

During this short lull, some GIs came across Norval in an open field, milking a cow and using his helmet as the bucket. The GIs had been told—by Norval himself, among others—not to drink any local milk, which was thought to cause tuberculosis. The troops who caught him in the act chided him gently, according to Robert Levy, who witnessed the incident, but my father was unchastened. Given the circumstances, he said, he was willing to take his chances.

Among the top field commanders in Normandy, there was some dissatisfaction with the Twenty-ninth Division's progress a week after D-Day. They had hoped the division would be in the city of St.-Lô by now, but instead it was bogged down 5 miles away, its casualties heavy in the week of fighting. On June 14 the First Battalion was assigned a new and, headquarters hoped, a more aggressive commander—Maj. Glover S. Johns Jr. A new offensive was in the works.

On the morning of June 16 the men of the 115th Regiment rose early and prepared to attack Les Foulons as part of the Twenty-ninth Division's renewed push for

St.-Lô. But the order to move forward was slow in coming, and the troops of the First Battalion remained in place until nearly nightfall because the Third Battalion, ahead of them, was bogged down at Les Foulons. Casualties from sniper fire continued to pour into the aid station, and Norval treated several wounded soldiers that morning.

In the afternoon he dashed off two quick letters, one to his parents and one to Fernie. To his parents he candidly admitted that the fighting left him anxious and afraid:

> We have had a few terrible experiences in this battalion and quite a few of us are shaken up. I have never been so nervous and frightened in my life, yet we are able to push on. This is D-9, or the 10th day of the invasion & progress seems satisfactory. Some of my aid men have been killed or wounded. . . . I have had bullets all around me, but my luck is good. My men have shown admirable courage & heroism in removing wounded while under fire. My health is excellent. . . .
> Save some of the newspapers for me to read when I get home. . . . Take good care of Fernie & the boys.

He told his wife that he had not had a single hour "of freedom from the sounds of gunfire since landing & it sure gets on one's nerves."

> Today we are resting in an orchard & things are fairly quiet, but snipers are 100 yards south of us & I have treated 6 gunshot wounds this morning. Bullets zing night & day, but fortunately the Luftwaffe have been prevented from coming over us except on the nights of D-Day and D-2.

Sweetheart, I haven't been able to dream about you since being here. It seems that when I fall asleep that it is so sound I don't dream at all & I miss that connection with you. When I do waken I am all alert at once to the environment & I miss those twilight states of thinking of home.

Excuse this writing 'cause I am in a foxhole with the letter on a water-can. I have collected a few souvenirs so far from the German dead. They are really well-equipped. Their dead outnumber ours. But it is a very sad and distressing thing to see (& smell) so many mangled men. It seems to be so useless for nations to do such things to each other.

At five o'clock in the morning of June 17, after further skirmishing, Les Foulons finally fell. The Americans pressed the attack, with the First Battalion marching through hedgerow country toward the area of Bois de Bretel, ever closer to St.-Lô. Resistance was heavy. One soldier wrote, "Captain Carter during the heat of battle was ever present with the dead and wounded." Norval spent part of the day with Chester Adams, the litter bearer he had encouraged on the beach during D-Day. While they were taking a pause under a tree, my father pulled out his wallet and showed Adams pictures of Tom and me. "I'd sure like to be home now with my boys," he said.

An orchard separated the American hedgerow from a German hedgerow. After a long and bloody afternoon of combat, the sun was beginning to set, and twilight descended on the battlefield. From the orchard, a no-man's land between the two positions, came the cries of the wounded. Two medics were there, tending to several casualties. Norval, on the front lines, was with E.J. Hamill behind a hedgerow next to a road when they heard the cries for help. My father prepared to move out from his cover to tend to the soldiers, but Hamill tried to persuade him to stay where he was. There were German snipers in the area, Hamill warned.

"I would help them, too," Norval said.

The medics who had been in the orchard came back for help in retrieving the casualties. Norval went with them to help one of the wounded soldiers, lying along the edge of the road, who had been shot in both feet and the stomach while scouting the German position beyond the hedgerow earlier in the day. As he examined the soldier, he cautioned the medics that it was too dangerous to call up litter bearers to bring the casualties back to the aid station.

Norval checked the soldier's wounds and reassured him, and then he and the medics turned to treat another casualty less than 10 feet away.

Hidden in the woods across the road was a German sniper with an automatic weapon. He had the men in his sights.

A burst of gunfire rang out. Bullets tore into the torso of Dr. Norval Carter of Huntington, West Virginia—captain in the US Army, only child of Eustace and Sapho Carter, husband of Fernie, father of two boys. He died at the edge of that orchard in Normandy, eleven days after landing on Omaha Beach. The two medics with him also died.

Did the man who killed my father see his Red Cross armbands? Did he purposely take aim and fire on three noncombatants who were simply tending to wounded soldiers? Or, in the twilight, could he not distinguish him from any other American GI who dared to venture into that orchard?

When the men of the First Battalion heard of his death, some of them swore they would find and kill the sniper. Only Captain Ryan's order kept them behind the hedgerow. In his book *The Clay Pigeons of St.-Lô*, the battalion's new commander, Major Johns, recalled learning of Norval's death. He was as furious as his men. "For God's sake, what was the Doc doing where a sniper could get him?" Johns demanded. "And why would a sniper be shooting a medic? He had his armband on, didn't he?"

Yes, he had his armband on. But he was dead all the same.

At the chateau Odette Pagny was making pastry when some American soldiers told her that Captain Carter had been killed. She was stunned. "I never thought one man like him could be hurt," she wrote a few months later.

My father was buried in a temporary cemetery near La Cambe and was posthumously awarded the Silver Star, Bronze Star, and Purple Heart. Odette Pagny's family tended his grave, and her niece Jacqueline bedecked it with flowers.

Life without Dad

7 Tom and I were eagerly awaiting the arrival of summer, while our mother tried to distract herself from her worries. The news was filled with accounts from the battlefields of northern France. All was going well, we were assured. The Allies were pushing forward, slowly but relentlessly. The Germans were falling back from the coast. Hitler's Fortress Europe had been breached, and even violent storms in the English Channel could not stop the British-American buildup on beaches so dearly secured on D-Day.

For millions of Americans like Fernie, the news reports from France lacked the single bit of information that mattered more than anything else: Is my husband still alive? Is my son lying in a foxhole, bleeding, with no one to care for him? Is my father fighting for his life, right now? Is my brother a prisoner? As they read about the fighting and listened to the radio, they had to wonder: Is he there? Is he safe? Will I ever see him again?

Norval came to Fernie in a dream, silent but smiling. He came nearer and nearer until his presence overwhelmed her. Then she awoke and sat up, crying and shaking. Aunt Becky, her older sister, heard Fernie's anguish from the other room and rushed to her. Fernie told her about the dream. The date was June 17, 1944.

About two weeks later, on July 1, she received his letters of June 13 and June 16, the first since his last letter from England on May 24. She was overjoyed—he had survived D-Day and the days of fighting that had followed. She immediately wrote back:

> Your letters of June 13 & 16 arrived this morning & they were like a drink of water to a man caught in the desert & dying of thirst. I felt a load being lifted immediately from my shoulders. I really believe I am the happiest person in Huntington, just to know that you were still ok, Sugar. I don't know why I love you so much but I sho' do, & always will. I hope by this time that you have been sent to a rest area because I know all of you must need it.

Then, on July 6, came the telegram. Not long afterward, Fernie's last four letters arrived at our house in Huntington, stamped "Return to Sender."

My mother's grief was, and still is, unimaginable. She left no record of her suffering and allowed her children no more than a passing glimpse of her pain. For our sake, she put on a brave show of being steady and dependable. Some advised her to give voice to her sorrow rather than repress it. "You haven't let your grief out at all," a friend wrote that summer. "It is easier on others that way, but it is mighty hard on you, and it just eats on you like a sore. If you could cry and carry on like a real baby just once, I think you would be better off. . . . I marvel that you have been so contained, but I don't think it is good for you."

Others offered the opposite advice. Her family, friends, and community pressured her to keep her chin up, saying that a stoic approach would make her husband proud and set a good example for her sons. In one of the many condolence letters that poured in, a friend of Norval's counseled that "you must be brave, must try not to be bitter, and while needing comfort yourself [you] must comfort Norval's parents."

She almost never let us see these burdens. Years later I learned from friends and family that she was inconsolable. My father's picture remained on her bureau and his image dominated our life as a family, but my mother rarely spoke of him. There was no scar—only an open wound that would never heal. As a four-year-old living in a child's world of toys, games, and friends, I could not appreciate my mother's pain. Indeed, I could barely comprehend that I would never see my father again.

Like other spouses and parents of soldiers killed in

action, my mother clung to the faint hope that the news was some bureaucratic mistake, no more real than the dream she had on June 17. She wrote to the War Department in Washington, asking for information about her husband's death. In a letter from Washington dated July 10, Maj. Gen. J. A. Ulio, the adjutant general, confirmed my father's death but said that no further information was available. Letters from Norval's comrades dispelled all hopes, but they also offered the consolation that he had not suffered. In a letter written "somewhere in France" on August 12, the battalion's commanding officer, Lt. Col. Glover Johns, offered more details.

> Captain Carter had gone forward to treat wounded men who were somewhat behind the very furthest lines—yet still under fire from snipers and an occasional undiscovered machine gun. I had warned him not to do this, but he was so intent on rendering really necessary medical aid to severely wounded men that he placed too much faith in his Red Cross brassard and got too far out in front—thinking only of our boys and never of himself. He was actually attending a badly wounded man whose life I am confident his early attention saved, when a sniper hit him squarely. He suffered not at all and if they ever get me, I should like to go as he did.
>
> Carter was in every real, true sense of the word, a hero. That is small satisfaction to you because you (and we) knew that anyway. But he gave his life for his fellow man, and the sniper who destroyed him robbed the world of a lifetime of splendid work—he would have saved countless others.
>
> I had known him only for a few days . . . but he had already become a close friend and instantly, on meet-

ing him, I had known I would have no worries with my medical section and that my boys would have the very finest care.

Colonel Johns closed by noting that he had several friends in Huntington who would testify that he was not one to offer "empty praise." Like his men on the front line, he was enraged that the enemy had fired on a noncombatant. In the weeks after Norval's death, he said, he had shot several "unscrupulous" enemy soldiers "for Carter."

Sapho Carter wrote a brief letter of thanks to another officer who had responded to Fernie's inquiries. Describing her son to the officer, she offered a glimpse of the pain in her heart.

> No one except parents, wife, and family understands or feels this terrible loss. We believe you, when you write of how he was loved, and of the devotion that existed between him and his comrades. From childhood on up through life he always had great sympathy for others and would go beyond his strength to help when needed. That's a great consolation. He lived a fully happy life in his thirty-two years; his married life could not have been more happy having his dear little boys....
>
> We hope and pray that some day when this terrible [war] is won, that you may come and see us in our home, that we may be able to understand and hear more about the passing of our dear boy Norval.

Throughout the summer, as the Allies pushed south and west of St.-Lô and Caen, Fernie received many letters, some from friends who had known her and Norval when they were childhood sweethearts. His best friend from those days, Chuck Elliott, who now lived in Kansas City, regretted that he was "too far away" to offer much help. But his words were honest and comforting. "This is not an easy letter to write, Fernie, for my cut is deep, too," he wrote. "You and the boys have a hard row . . . with a shining star above to look to when the going gets tough. No words can replace Norval, nor lighten the loss to you and the boys, nor to me. He died doing his job for all of us, a good man, a *real* man, and a good job, because that was his way."

In a separate letter to Tom and me, the man who signed himself "Uncle Chuck" offered advice he knew would mean more to us when we were older:

> The last time I saw you, we had a good old rough-house like your Daddy and I used to have years ago. Now your Daddy has been killed while helping our soldiers in France, and he can't come back to rough-house with you, or be a pal to you like he was before he left and like he was to me.
>
> You fellas have a big job to do—a job that only real men can handle—and your Daddy would not have risked and lost his life for us all if he didn't know you had the stuff in you to do your job well, as he did.
>
> Your first job is to help your mother in every way you can while you are growing up because she has to do the whole job of being mother and daddy, and making a home for you. You will help her most by always being kind to her, and to others, and helping in any way you can to keep your own parts of your house in order. Protect your mother from sorrow, and don't do anything to disappoint her.

The other part of your job is to grow to be the men your Daddy wanted you to be—and as much like him as you can. Be always clean and honest, to yourselves and to others. Do good things for each other and don't fight any more than you have to. Look out for each other, help each other, and you will have a happy life.

The greatest thing you can do to honor your Daddy is to be as fine as he was and make your mother proud of you. . . . Remember always that he gave his life to help others, and was always doing good things for other people.

By war's end, tens of thousands of women across the country were in my mother's position—war widows, left to carry on their lives as best they could, brokenhearted and lonely. America's 400,000 dead soldiers left behind an estimated 183,000 children who would live the rest of their lives as I have—with only a memory, perhaps not even that, of a father who gave his life for his country.

I do not remember my mother reading Uncle Chuck's words to me, but I behaved as if I had. As I grew older, I tried to protect my mother from reminders of her grief. When friends came over to my house to play and asked where my father was and what he did, I quickly shushed them. Occasionally I failed. Once, when I was in junior high school, my mother and I went to a movie, a light comedy about a mother and father trying to raise a large family. Toward the end the family gathered at the college graduation of the youngest child. The camera moved from face to face—from sibling to sibling, their spouses and children next to them, and then to the aging faces of the parents, wistful but happy. I glanced over at my mother and saw that she was crying. Trying to comfort her, I blurted out something like, "Oh, you don't have to cry." She waved me away with a sharp downward swat of her hand and told me to leave her alone. She must have been reflecting on her own struggle to raise two children without a husband and the sad reality that she would never share the joys of our growing up, our graduations and weddings, and the births of grandchildren.

On another occasion we were invited to dinner at the home of an older couple. Our host told some anecdotes about his experiences during World War I, funny stories that made war seem like summer camp. My mother laughed with him and the others, but it was a superficial laugh, one she often used to get past unpleasant topics. Heading home after dinner, I said something about war not sounding so bad. She snapped back in an uncharacteristically angry voice: "Damn! How dare he talk that way to me! *He* came back!"

Despite our loss, mine was not an unhappy childhood. I grew up in comfortable circumstances, thanks in part to the life insurance policy my father had bought during basic training at Camp Pickett. The mortgage on our house was paid off by the insurance money, so my mother did not have that worry in addition to her other concerns. The house was substantial: it had a kitchen, breakfast den, dining room, living room, and powder room on the first floor; three bedrooms, a den, and a bathroom on the second floor, and a full room with a bath on the attic floor. The small back yard was sufficient for a truncated badminton court and flower gardens along the edges. The two-car garage held bicycles, lawn chairs, garden tools—and Norval's beloved Chevy convertible, which my mother drove until around 1953, when it simply gave out. We lived in a desirable section of the city, a short walk from a large park. We ate well, had all the clothes we needed, and never suffered a lack of toys, books, or friends. I had private music lessons, first with Aunt Becky, who taught me piano, and later trombone lessons from a Marshall College faculty member. Tom and I both had two years of ballroom dance lessons and went to summer camp. We took vacations to Washington, DC, and the Chesapeake Bay.

Despite these advantages, I envied kids in the neighborhood who had fancier toys and took more exotic vacations than we did. Although far from dominating my life, my envy lasted through high school and college. I disdained that exclusive group of country-club kids who went off to private prep schools, especially when my girlfriend, the daughter of a doctor who was a former colleague of my father's, joined them. I attended Swarthmore College in Pennsylvania on a scholarship financed by the college, the US government's war orphans benefits program, and a loan from the Norval Carter Memorial Scholarship Fund, established by my father's medical colleagues in Huntington. Many students at Swarthmore came from wealthier families; they had attended private schools and had traveled extensively. In my view they had what I wanted because they had fathers and I did not.

The photograph of his father that Walter Ford carried in his pocket in sixth grade.

I also sensed that my disadvantage would have implications for the future. I anticipated that I would have to support not only my own family, if I had one, but also my mother. I talked with my brother about my moving back to Huntington after college to take care of her. Tom assured me that she could take care of herself and wanted us to lead our own lives, but I was not so certain.

My envy diminished as I grew older, but my sadness did not. They were there all along, disguised by more obvious resentments. In the first year or two after my father's death, I occasionally imagined that he might yet walk in the front door, having been lost rather than killed. I brooded over the framed photographs and the snapshots in photograph albums. Toward the end of my grade-school days I found a small photograph of him. Along its bottom edge I wrote "Dad" and kept the picture in my shirt pocket. At times when I was alone, I stared longingly at the picture.

Like my mother, I maintained a stoic public face. The only time I remember showing my grief was when I was in sixth grade. My teacher was telling the class, all of us old enough to remember the war and its sacrifices, about my father. He was a much-loved doctor, she said, and had served his country with bravery. She had seen him shortly before he left for the army, and he had told her that he might not come back, might never see his family again. Sitting at my desk, I started to cry. I attempted to hide behind a book, but the teacher saw my tears and allowed me to leave. I ran the two blocks to our house. My mother asked why I was upset. Looking pained, she gently comforted me, saying, "Yes, sometimes it is very hard to keep going."

I was always proud of my father. If anyone asked about him, I said he was a doctor who was killed in the war while trying to rescue a wounded soldier. Many of my teachers knew him—some had been his patients— and invariably expressed affection and admiration for him. I welcomed these comments, because they gave me new bits of information or confirmed impressions I already had, helping me build an image of him: a

well-liked man, a respected doctor, a devoted husband, a practical joker with a zany sense of humor—a
lovable hero.

While Tom and I were growing up, most of the
adults around us were women. My mother was
the center of that world. At bedtime she read to us or
invented stories. She cared for me when I was sick,
attended events at school and church, took me to
Saturday afternoon football games, and encouraged my
music lessons. She was always there for us (she did not
work outside the home until I was in junior high school;
eventually she worked for the March of Dimes, the
Marshall College Artist Series, and the Girl Scouts). We
were proud of her, just as we were proud of our father—
proud of her ability to draw and paint and to play both
the piano and the violin.

Three other women nurtured and supported us.
Rarely a day went by without our seeing Aunt Becky,
Fernie's unmarried sister who was twelve years older and
a music teacher in a public junior high school. It was family lore that Becky once had a serious suitor but that she
discouraged the relationship out of a sense of obligation
to her widowed mother, Anna Lowry, and to Fernie. Since
Anna's death in 1940, Becky had lived with my great-aunt
Minnie Zittel Noel, a childless widow and good-natured
soul who loved playing games with me, particularly
Chinese checkers. She too was a musician and often took
out her violin—or fiddle, as she called it—to play Stephen
Foster melodies and country dance tunes.

When Aunt Minnie fell ill in the late 1950s, after I

left for college, she and Becky moved in with Fernie and remained with her as they aged. I once complained to Tom that our mother was overburdened with caring for a succession of older relatives, but he thought it was good for her, and he was probably right. My mother said she had lived her life in service to her family and had no regrets.

The other important woman in my life was Sapho Carter—Granny, as we called her. A large, strong woman and a tireless talker, she liked to give the impression that she was in charge. She always greeted me and Tom with smothering hugs and was very strict about our having clean hands and faces. I often felt constrained in her presence. Granny was perhaps overly protective of my mother. Once, when a man asked my mother out to dinner not long after my father's death, Granny called him and told him to stay away from Fernie because she had children to look after and no time for dating. When my mother told us the story years later, she laughed about it and it became a family joke. I got the idea that she did not think the fellow measured up, anyway. Nevertheless, I was glad that a strange man had not intruded into our small family circle.

Tom did not seem as close to these women as I did; he was more independent and focused on people outside the family. He was like Norval and even looked like him, with his red hair. When our father died, Tom stopped playing the piano and took up Dad's instrument, the clarinet. Early on, possibly as early as grade school, he had declared his intention to become a doctor, and in high school, in imitation of Dad, he began smoking a pipe. Like Norval, he liked to wear unusual hats—a cowboy hat or a Sherlock Holmes–style cap. Sometimes Fernie recognized her husband in one of the pranks we pulled. "That's just like your Dad," she would say. Tom and I liked to hear that.

When he was sixteen, Tom married his high school sweetheart, Susan Starr—like Norval and Fernie, they eloped. She became pregnant not long after they were married, and Tom was a father before he graduated from high school. They named their son Thomas Norval. Our mother was bitterly disappointed in Tom, not so much from a moral perspective but because she thought marriage and parenthood would hinder his chance for a full life, personally and professionally. With support from our family and Susan's, Tom finished high school and went on to Marshall College and then, without finishing his degree, to the Medical College of Virginia. He even received a recommendation from Dr. Walter Vest.

Although Tom and I were surrounded by women, there were two important men in our lives: our grandfather and Dr. John Morris.

After retiring from the railroad in 1946, Eustace Carter had more time to spend with Tom and me, and we loved being with him. Sometimes we would sit on the front porch of my grandparents' second-floor apartment and watch the cars go by, keeping track of their colors (most cars were black at the time). While I was still in grade school, he took me on the train to Cincinnati to see a Reds baseball game, a huge treat.

The other prominent man in our lives was Norval's

friend from boyhood and medical school, John Morris. I could not get enough of him. Our families often ate dinner together on Saturday nights, and we took several vacations together in Virginia. I often accompanied him to the local high school and college track meets that he loved. Being with him, even in his old age, felt like being with my father. Other men in the community occasionally took me along on expeditions, often to ball games or circuses, and men from our church took me to father-son dinners.

I looked up to several of my male Sunday school teachers, and the language of the church services and Sunday school lessons mingled with my thoughts of my father: "Our father, who art in Heaven"; "Thy Father's will"; "Thy Father's love." Whenever I heard or read references to God as the Father, I thought of Dad. I had the feeling that, like God, he was looking down at me benignly, and I sensed that his spirit was there in the church. I gradually took religion more seriously and became active in the church, as did Tom. We each wanted to do God's will and felt we were called to do something great because we were the sons of a very special father. I thought I might become a minister. Later those feelings gave way to a more secular outlook, but the motivation to serve others remained.

When I was in the homes of friends who had fathers, I reacted with mixed emotions. The deep, masculine voices, the air of strength and authority were both intimidating and attractive. If a friend's father was playful and good-humored, I felt happy and comfortable; if he seemed stern or harsh, I felt afraid. I was always looking or listening to see or hear what this large male would do or say, well aware that this presence was lacking at my house.

That uneasiness continued into my college years. During my junior year, on my first acquaintance with Bonnie's family in Vermont, my future father-in-law made a vivid impression. He was a tall, strong man with a solid bass voice and a presence that commanded attention. He was kindly, courteous, and well spoken. I was struck by his role in the house—he was very much the head of an affectionate family who looked up to him. He had stature in the community as well: After starting his career as a teacher in a one-room school, he eventually served as state commissioner of education.

When Bonnie and I had children of our own, I felt unsure about how to be a father—how to discipline them, how to convey values to them by word and deed, how to teach skills and develop abilities. I took our children to see musical and theater performances, as my mother had done for me. I tried to promote core values—taking responsibility for one's actions and not inflicting unjust or unnecessary harm on others. Our children have turned out well, but my lack of confidence gave me anxious moments along the way.

My brother and I celebrated our graduations together in 1962. I earned my bachelor's degree in history from Swarthmore that June, just as Tom—now the father of three boys—was graduating from medical school. We both moved to the Boston area, Tom to take an internship at Tufts University's New England Medical Center and I as a graduate student at

Tufts' Fletcher School of Law and Diplomacy. We saw each other often, and Tom was my best man when Bonnie and I married in Vermont that December.

Tom continued to follow where our father had led. He had joined a US Army program that paid part of his medical school expenses in return for a commitment of eight years of active duty. After his internship at Tufts, he was sent to an army hospital in Denver for three years of residency. (In the meantime I transferred to a doctoral program in economics at the University of Rochester in upstate New York; I never finished my dissertation.) Tom told me he had felt that he had no choice but to be a doctor, that he had to take Norval's place. If he had a chance to start over again, he said, he would have done something else. I was surprised—I did not think anyone had put that kind of pressure on Tom or me.

After his residency Tom requested a two-year tour in Vietnam. I thought Tom was carrying his imitation of Norval too far. I feared he would find his way to the front line and take risks that no father of three children should take. In fact, in his position as chief of the department of medicine, Twenty-fourth Evacuation Hospital, he did come under enemy fire on more than one mission and had at least one close call, when a helicopter lifted him from an evacuation site being overrun by the North Vietnamese. Tom made it home, however, and served the rest of his military service at Fort Wainwright in Fairbanks, Alaska. The only casualty was his marriage; Susan and the boys moved to Columbus, Ohio.

Like Norval, Tom had little patience with military bureaucracy. When his obligation ended, he went into private practice in Alaska, which he had grown to love. He took up painting and raced sled dogs. Like many citizens of that vast state, Tom soon got a pilot's license.

In the late afternoon of February 11, 1972, Tom took off from Fairbanks in his four-seater Bellanca airplane to attend a professional meeting out of state. He planned to fly to Massachusetts after that, to visit Bonnie and me and see his new red-haired niece—our daughter, Catherine. He would complete his trip east by flying to Huntington.

Tom had been scheduled to fly earlier in the day, but a mechanical problem delayed his departure by several hours. Rather than postpone his trip by a day, he took off as soon as the plane was fixed, late in the winter afternoon. Light snow showers were forecast for the area, and visibility was low. Tom had only limited experience flying on instruments and through clouds. Nevertheless, he was determined to get going. His flight plan called for him to follow the Alaska Highway to his first destination, Whitehorse, in Canada's Yukon Territory.

He never arrived.

My mother called me the next day to tell me that Tom was missing. I had not heard her voice so shaky and full of grief since that day in 1944 when I had interrupted her to ask if I could go outside to play. A few days later, Tom's two older sons and I flew to Canada to join the rescue effort, while their younger brother remained in Ohio with Susan. The boys were convinced that their dad was alive in the snow and ice of the Yukon. I was not nearly so optimistic. I left the Yukon on February 24 and returned to my mother. The search was called off the next day.

With Aunt Becky and Bonnie beside her, I told my

mother the details of the search and also what others had told me, that pilots had been known to reappear in the spring after surviving a winter crash. "We'll just have to wait and see," I said. She shrank into her chair, just as she had twenty-eight years earlier when the telegram arrived.

Tom's remains were finally discovered in August 1974. He was considerably off course when he crashed, some 40 miles north of Whitehorse. An investigation concluded that he had "encountered reduced visibility in snow or cloud. His reaction would be to reverse heading to regain visual flight conditions. In doing so, the aircraft evidently entered a spiral dive from which the pilot was unable to recover prior to impact with the ground." On top of the poor flying conditions and his inexperience, he had deviated from his flight plan in unfamiliar territory. Tom was both reckless and unlucky—like his father. He was thirty-four years old.

B onnie and I had moved to Newton, Massachusetts, in the summer of 1971, after my four years as an instructor in economics at Hobart College. I was working as a research economist at Charles River Associates, a consulting firm in Cambridge. My career seemed to be on track. My supervisors were pleased with my work, and I received a raise after six months with the firm. The children were a great joy. Norman was nearly four years old when Tom was killed, and Catherine was not quite a year old. They filled our house with laughter.

In the months following Tom's death, however, I began to make mistakes on the job. I was working hard, often late into the evening and on weekends, but the harder I tried, the less I seemed to accomplish. I was not sleeping well. A year after Tom's death, I received a harsh performance review. It included my own critical evaluation. I heard later that when the firm's president read my self-evaluation, he was disturbed by my low self-esteem. He suggested that I see a therapist.

I had never seen myself as in need of therapy, but I made an appointment. At the first session I told the therapist I was there to deal with job performance issues, but in answering a question about my family history, as I talked about Tom's disappearance and my father's death, tears welled up. At the time I was not aware that there was any connection between grief and work performance.

The following Saturday, I was in the kitchen fixing breakfast for Norman and Catherine. Norman was gleeful because I was going to be home all day (I usually went to the office on Saturdays), although I would have to spend it working in my room. Norman said he would peek in from time to time because he liked me so much. At this remark I experienced a surge of affection and sorrow. I loved my son and enjoyed our relationship; I felt grief for Tom and Dad, whose relationships with their children ended so terribly. My life and the lives of my brother and father were becoming entangled in my mind.

I had been in therapy for a month when the firm's president summoned me to his office and told me to look for work elsewhere. I felt as if I had been kicked in the stomach. I was not consciously angry at my bosses—I knew my work was unsatisfactory—but I felt worthless and hopeless. Everything seemed to be falling apart. I was about to be out of work at the age of thirty-three, and I feared that I would not be able to support my family. Coming home from work on the bus that day, I looked out the window and saw some children riding bicycles. I thought gloomily that I would not be able to offer my children this simple pleasure.

I continued with therapy during the summer of 1973 while looking for work. In November I found a job with Data Resources Inc. (DRI), an economics information company, providing data and forecasts on the US steel industry. I plunged into the job and worked hard—more late nights and weekends. Often I felt as if I was barely hanging on, but I persevered. My goal was simply to provide for my family and make it to retirement. My adolescent desire to do great things for society—the reason I went to the Fletcher School after graduating from Swarthmore—gave way to more practical concerns. But I could never shake the feeling that something would go wrong, that I would somehow fail. One night, driving home very late from work, I had a vivid impression of my father and Tom. Their faces seemed to be side by side in the darkened sky, and they were smiling, as if checking in on me. "Hi, Dad. Hi, Tom," I said. "I'm doing okay. I think I'm going to make it." I was later promoted to vice president and then principal of DRI.

More than a decade after I started therapy, in 1985—the forty-first anniversary of D-Day, the forty-first anniversary of my father's death—I decided to visit Normandy.

Bonnie and Catherine flew with me to France; Norman was already there, participating in a high school student exchange program. I was hoping to retrace my father's steps, so I asked my mother for any information she had about his time there. For the first time she showed me the letters she had received from Odette Pagny, the Frenchwoman whose family's chateau had been converted into an evacuation site in 1944. The letters offered details of my father's last days.

If my mother's willingness to show me Odette's letters was a signal that she was willing to talk more about my father, I passed on the opportunity. I still believed that pressing her for information would only cause more pain for both of us.

After meeting Norman in Paris, we drove to Normandy. I knew my father was buried in the American cemetery on the bluffs of Omaha Beach. We arrived on a chilly, rainy day to find row upon row of crosses and stars of David in an expanse of beautifully maintained open space. As we moved among the graves of those thousands of young Americans, I struggled for composure. We finally found Norval's grave at the far end of the cemetery.

When I touched his marker, I felt a current of connection with him. "Here I am, Dad," I thought. "I've finally come to you." More than forty years after I last saw him, we were reunited. "I had not known what to expect," I later wrote my mother. "I felt my emotion building as we approached the cemetery—I saw troops everywhere—and when we drove in view of the graves, I was overcome by the sight of all those white crosses. It is easy to see in those crosses the form of people, with arms outstretched. My feelings at seeing Dad's headstone were the strongest I can remember. . . . It seemed that this was the end of a long journey, and a reunion."

I wanted to visit the beach, but because of the rain we drove on to Pointe du Hoc, where specially trained Rangers had scaled a sheer cliff, under fire, to knock out a strategic German position on D-Day. We tried to trace our way through the back roads of rural Normandy, looking for the chateau where my father spent some of his last days. Local people in a tavern told us that Odette Pagny had died but that her sister-in-law, Danielle, lived across the street.

Danielle was home, along with her loud and excited dog, and although she spoke no English, she welcomed us. Bonnie and Norman, both of whom spoke some French, told her about our journey. Her daughter, then very ill in Paris, was Jacqueline, who as a young girl, forty years ago, had put flowers on my father's grave before his remains were transferred to the permanent American cemetery. Danielle gave us directions to the chateau, not far away. We found it—a large, attractive house in very good condition—but a locked gate kept us from exploring any further.

The next day we drove back to my father's grave, walked around the cemetery, and trooped down a path leading to Omaha Beach. We lingered there, looking up at the hill that must have been so terrifying in 1944. Try as I might, I could not imagine the scenes of that day: well-armed Germans firing from the hills, the Allied soldiers struggling to make it across the beach.

At this time I still knew little about my father, apart from the family history, summed up in one sentence: "He was shot by a sniper while trying to rescue a wounded soldier on the battlefield in France." I was frustrated by my inability to convey to my wife and children what he was like, how people felt about him, or the importance of his story. They could see that I had been profoundly moved by visiting his grave and the places where he had been in combat, but it all must have seemed mysterious. They did not ask much about him. They held the same assumption that I held about my mother—that the subject was too painful to discuss. I interpreted the children's reticence as adolescent indifference to serious issues, particularly those related to their parents.

Back in Newton, I knew I had to tell my mother about the trip. Visiting my father's grave was no routine vacation, and I spent hours composing a letter. Some months later, on a business trip, I stopped in Huntington to see her. We sat together, looking through the Normandy photographs. As I showed her the ones taken in the cemetery, she sat quietly, with her hands in her lap and something of a wistful smile. I tried to be pleasantly nonchalant. When we had finished looking at the photographs, I excused myself to go to the bathroom—and that broke the tension. When I returned, she said something like, "Those are very nice pictures. It looks like you all had a very nice trip." There was no further discussion. We were back to our standard operating procedure: We did not talk about our loss.

When my mother died in 1995, all my family connections to my childhood were severed. My father, my grandfather Carter, Aunt Minnie, Tom, my grandmother Carter, Aunt Becky, and now my mother—all were gone. In the summer and fall of 1995, as I began to go through the letters I had brought back from

Huntington, I felt in turmoil again. I had mental images of my parents and Tom, sometimes singly, sometimes together. I associated them with some of my favorite music—particularly Anton Bruckner's string quintet, choral motets, and symphonies, especially his eighth, with its themes of grief, solace, and affirmation. I slept erratically and found it difficult to concentrate on my work. I occasionally did nothing more than stare out my office window.

That fall I turned to therapy again. Once again I found anger and sadness. I had not fully appreciated the connection between my losses and my distress, but I learned, slowly, that my resentment was not directed at Dad or Tom or Mom. I *was* resentful over how much I had lost, but I did not blame them. To me, they had been noble. They had just run into bad luck, which is more a matter of chance than of blame—my parents in the war, my brother in his accident. I felt deeply sorry for them. All the while I was becoming acquainted with my father through his letters, and he was becoming an almost tangible presence in my life. I began to realize that despite all the losses, to paraphrase something I read somewhere, love has left behind more than death has taken away. I have had the good fortune of a loving family, both as a child and with my own family as an adult. Although the child within me is still sad and angry, the man in me knows that in death my father showed me—and others— everything I need to know about courage and sacrifice and the awful price we are sometimes called upon to pay for liberty. My mother, although she mourned every day of her life after receiving that telegram, taught me another lesson. Regardless of our circumstances, each of us must do what we can with the talents we have to bring some light into the darkness of the world. I was always proud of my father's service to his country and my mother's service to her family. But I did not truly understand what that word *service* meant.

Now I know. And with this knowledge and my belated sharing of his life I have found a measure of peace.

In January 1997, I came across a note written to myself in June 1994, when the news was filled with commemorations marking the fiftieth anniversary of D-Day. In a news clip I had caught the name of a Twenty-ninth Division veteran from nearby Fitchburg, Massachusetts. I had written down the man's name but had put it aside and never returned to it.

I called him, but he did not recognize my father's name. He had been in the 175th Regiment; Norval was in the 115th. But he encouraged me to contact the Twenty-ninth Division Association, which served, among many other functions, as a clearinghouse for inquiries about veterans. The group sent me its newsletter, which recommended several reference books that veterans' relatives had found useful in tracking down members of the division.

Excited about this promising new lead, I went to the local library on a Sunday afternoon and submitted a request for the books. I was then drawn to the stacks to see what other World War II books might be available. My eye caught the title of a book—*June 6, 1944: Voices of D-Day*, by Gerald Astor. I pulled it from the shelf and flipped through the pages. I found a section titled "Beyond Omaha."

And there I saw my father's name.

The book included the reminiscences of Frank Wawrynovic, a 115th Regiment veteran who had landed on Omaha Beach on D-Day. While on a scouting mission on June 17, he had been badly wounded but had managed to drag himself back toward the American front line. He had called out for help, and two medics responded. After checking him quickly, they went off to find litter bearers. When they returned, they were accompanied by Capt. Norval Carter, the battalion surgeon, who examined him and then turned his attention to a wounded soldier lying nearby. Shots rang out, and Captain Carter and the two medics fell to the ground. "These men had answered my call for help and died on account of me," Wawrynovic had written. "To them I owe a debt I can never repay."

Frank Wawrynovic was the man my father had tried to save, the wounded soldier of our family legend. I reread the passage several times. It gave details I had never known. I had a first-hand account of my father's death.

The book listed Frank's hometown as Clearfield, Pennsylvania. I rushed home, called information, and got his number. I dialed the number and a woman's voice answered. I asked to speak with Frank. He was just coming in from the shop, I was told. After a short pause, a man's voice came on the line. I asked him if he was the person mentioned in Gerald Astor's book. He replied that he was.

"I'm the son of Captain Carter," I said.

Journey's End

8

Frank J. Wawrynovic was born in 1917, one of six children of Polish immigrants who had settled in the coal-mining town of Osceola Mills in central Pennsylvania. As a boy during the Great Depression, Frank helped put food on the family's table by hunting and fishing. After graduating from high school in 1935, he worked for a year with the Civilian Conservation Corps, building roads, dams, and bridges. Then, like so many other young men in his town, he went to work in the mines.

For six years he worked on his back in the cold, narrow seams, chipping away at the coal overhead as water dripped on him incessantly. It was brutal labor. Like so

Frank Wawrynovic after completion of special training with the Twenty-ninth Division Provisional Ranger Battalion, England, 1943.

many others, Frank seemed destined to a lifetime in the mines, finally emerging—if he survived—broken in health, an old man before his time. There must be a better way, Frank thought. There must be a better life.

The war lifted him out of the pit. Not long after Pearl Harbor he was drafted, and within a few months the young coal miner was training for war with the Twenty-ninth Division in England. He showed promise, bravery, and leadership. He volunteered for, and was accepted into, the Twenty-ninth Division Provisional Ranger Battalion, an elite unit. After intensive training in Scotland, the Rangers were reintegrated into the division.

On June 6, 1944, Frank landed with C Company, First Battalion, 115th Regiment, on Omaha Beach. He scrambled across the beach, strewn with human and mechanical wreckage, and reached the bluffs. As the division pushed inland, Frank's hunting skills and his Ranger training earned him the risky assignment of forward scout. He moved ahead of the American front line, probing and scouting the German defenses, eliminating enemy gunners when he encountered them.

Frank had reconciled himself to grim reality: It was simply a matter of time before he would be wounded or killed. Hidden behind the hedgerows, the Germans were lying in wait for GIs like himself to move forward into open fields. Some young German with a machine gun would open fire, and there would be no possibility of escape. Frank hoped that the bullets, when they came, would not tear through his stomach. He dreaded being shot in the stomach.

After the landings Frank's thoughts often focused on his mother. He feared more for her than for himself. He had accepted the inevitability of injury or death for himself, a single man, but he hated the thought of the pain and grief his mother would experience. Life had not been easy for her, rearing six children in a coal-mining town during the Depression. He had not seen her in nearly two years, and he wished, more than anything, that they could see each other again.

On June 17 Frank was moving through an apple orchard separating the Americans, who were ready to advance from their hedgerow on the east, from the Germans, who were behind a hedgerow at the far end of the orchard. Frank was moving along the edge of the orchard, close to a hedgerow that ran along the side of a narrow country road. A few other Americans, widely spaced to his left, also were advancing through the orchard. Machine guns opened fire, and several of the GIs fell instantly. Frank hit the dirt at the base of the hedgerow and lay still behind some weeds, knowing that the slightest movement would attract the enemy's attention. As he waited for the cover of darkness, he heard the cries of wounded Americans nearby. He wanted to come to their aid but knew that he could not—the Germans figured he was dead, and any movement would attract their attention.

Frank planned to wait until dark, throw a grenade over the German hedgerow, vault over the side hedgerow, and then dash across the road into the woods. But before Frank could escape, another soldier in the orchard, stricken by fear or panic, started running toward him. He was cut down, nearly falling on Frank as he collapsed. At that moment Frank made his move. He leaped to clear the shoulder-high hedgerow, but the German gunner had him in his sights. There was another burst of fire, and Frank was hit as he went over the hedgerow. He fell and lay motionless in a ditch beside the road, pretending to be dead.

Frank had been hit in both ankles and, as he had feared, in the stomach. His right leg seemed to be broken. He had neither his helmet nor his rifle—he had lost both as he vaulted over the hedgerow. Inch by inch, Frank crawled toward the American line, about 75 yards away. He was exhausted and was losing blood, but he dared not stop. If the Germans counterattacked, he was a dead man. Frank remembered once seeing a GI put a bayonet through a wounded German soldier and had never forgotten that soldier's frightful scream. Several hours later, Frank finally edged close to the American position. He had lost so much blood he feared he was dying. He called out for a medic.

Frank spoke hesitantly at first. The call from Capt. Norval Carter's son, completely unexpected, had thrown him off balance. More than a half century had passed since that day in Normandy when Captain Carter raced to his side to help him and paid for his bravery with his life.

For years Frank had intended to contact our family. He knew only that Captain Carter was from West Virginia—he did not know the town or city—and so when business took him there he visited local World War II monuments, looking for my father's name. But he never mounted an aggressive search to find us, partly because he did not have the time and partly because he was reluctant to reopen old wounds—his and ours.

A few days after our telephone conversation, Frank sent me a letter that expressed his gratitude to my father and all those who gave their lives so that we might live in a better world:

> After these many years it was a great surprise, even a shock, to hear from the son of the man who, after helping to pull many wounded men to safety, was killed as he came to help me and another wounded soldier as we

lay helpless in a ditch beside a hedgerow in Normandy. While I did not know your father personally at the time of his death, I feel that I have gotten to know him very well since then. As I grow older, I do not believe that a day goes by that I do not think of him and of the many other young men, especially of the friends that I had, that were killed in the battles of [World War II]. As a survivor, in spite of many personal hardships, I look back and see how really wonderful life can be. And knowing this, I can also see how it could have been for them and for their loved ones had not their lives been taken from them. What a great sacrifice your father and so many others were called upon to make! I have gone back to Normandy four times since the war (1984, 1987, 1993, and 1994). And I am planning to go back this year. I go back mostly to visit the graves of those whom I knew. I always stop at your father's grave.

I soon learned more about this man whom my father had attempted to save so many years ago. After my father and the two medics were killed, Frank dragged himself to the American hedgerow as darkness fell. Hearing the voices of GIs from behind it, he called out softly for help. He saw several Americans approaching, but their faces faded as he lost consciousness. Frank was brought to a field hospital and soon evacuated to England and then the States, spending a year and a half recovering from his wounds. He was discharged with a permanent disability—as well as a Bronze Star and Purple Heart.

When he returned home, the one-time coal miner enrolled at what was then called Pennsylvania State College. With the help of the GI bill, Frank earned a bachelor's degree in forestry and a master's degree in wildlife management. He married a young woman from his hometown, Stella Jedrziewski.

Frank and Stella were a lot like Norval and Fernie: They had known each other since they were children, lived across the street from each other, and married while still students. Both Frank and Stella came from Polish immigrant families, and both were veterans. Stella had served as an army nurse at Fort Meade, Maryland, where she cared mostly for wounded German prisoners.

They had three children, all of whom died in childhood or early adulthood. Their son Peter died at birth. Their son John, born in 1950, was diagnosed with leukemia at the age of three and died a year later. Their daughter, Barbara Jean, was born with cerebral palsy in 1952. Although seriously handicapped, Barbara Jean spent her short life—she died in 1969—not in an institution, a common practice at the time, but at home, with her loving and devoted parents.

Despite these unimaginable sorrows, Frank and Stella managed to keep going, drawing on strengths they did not know they had. They formed their own company, Utilities Forestry Services, to clear and maintain rights-of-way for power lines, pipelines, and other utility projects. They started small, with a crew consisting almost entirely of World War II veterans, two of whom, like Frank, had been wounded. Stella managed the home office and Frank ran the field operations. Eventually, they established a partnership with seven utility companies in the region and worked on state and local projects. They worked hard and prospered. Even into the late 1990s, when Frank was in his eighties, he rose before five o'clock in the morning to join work crews clearing paths for power lines through rural Pennsylvania. Eventually, he was forced to slow down. The wounds he suffered in Normandy had never fully healed, and Frank reluctantly accepted that he had entered what he called "a new stage in my life." In a letter to me he wrote:

> So many miles of walking in the woods, over so many hills, over so many years, have deformed my once wounded right leg so severely that even with an artificial brace, the distance that I can now walk is limited. And then there is the pain. But I would not have wanted it otherwise, for there have been many compensating rewards. High among these is doing hard and challenging work that I enjoyed in the outdoors, [which] helped to keep my mind away from the war and from the effects of [the] devastating loss of all three of our children at their early age.

With these losses never far from their minds, Frank and Stella found time for those in their community who also knew misfortune, tragedy, and limited opportunity. Over the years they made generous donations to local civic and veterans' groups. They contributed a million dollars to Pennsylvania State's College of Medicine, located in Hershey, to support research in leukemia and cerebral palsy. They quietly provided scholarship money for students in central Pennsylvania who wished to study either forestry or nursing. They gave money or company stock to their original employees or their surviving spouses to help them in their retirement. They supported their church, library, and fire department. And they helped fund memorials to fallen soldiers. In all their acts of giving, they were unobtrusive. They are humble and grateful people.

My father, too, believed that people are worth helping and that lives are worth saving, and the lives of Frank and Stella Wawrynovic bear him out. Frank said he owed him and the two medics "a debt that can never be repaid." But that debt has, in fact, been repaid a hundred times over. Frank and Stella's resiliency, determination, and generosity have improved the lives of countless neighbors, friends, and even strangers. They have helped the Carter family, too. Several years after I made contact with Frank, he and Stella donated $250,000 to the Norval Carter Memorial Medical Scholarship Fund at Marshall University in Huntington, a fund established by my father's colleagues years earlier.

Frank never forgot the sights, the sounds, and the sacrifices of war. In a short memoir, "A Soldier Remembers Normandy," he wrote:

> The war is not over for the combat survivor . . . when he leaves the battlefield, for he takes with him the mental and physical scars of war. . . . The passing of years does not erase the memories that are so deeply embedded in his mind. . . . A man shows his innermost feelings as he sheds a tear when he returns to visit the scenes of his former battles. . . . As he slowly walks alone among the rows upon rows of white crosses and stars, he grieves. . . . They are all with God now.
> Only he is the wanderer.

Frank at Norval's grave in Normandy on June 6, 1993, before his friendship with Captain Carter's son had begun.

Frank's memoir, published in the Twenty-ninth Division Association's newsletter in November 1991, was dedicated to my father and the two medics. In September 1997 my family and I joined Frank and other D-Day veterans for a visit to the hallowed ground of Normandy. Together we would pay tribute to fallen heroes.

When I first visited my father's grave in 1985, I had known very little about him. Now, through my parents' correspondence, my contact with people like Frank Wawrynovic, and my research into the Normandy campaign, I was better informed but still unprepared for the intensity of the experience. In that sprawling cemetery above Omaha Beach, I was deeply moved to witness these elderly soldiers as they solemnly paid respect to their fallen comrades. Some of these men had been with my father, and in their company I felt as if I were in his presence.

One of these was E. J. Hamill, the soldier who had begged my father to clear him for the D-Day invasion even though he was ill, had stood with him as their landing craft approached Omaha Beach, and had tried to dissuade him from venturing into the open to treat Frank and the other wounded soldiers. Hamill led my children and me down to the beach. "I was with your granddad when we landed on this beach," he told them.

Hamill pointed out the path they had taken up the hill overlooking the beach. It is unlike any other beach in the world. Although the place is tranquil now, vestiges of war and sacrifice are still evident. To the west the sheer cliffs of Pointe du Hoc lead to the well-preserved bunkers that the Rangers attacked on D-Day. The bluffs above Omaha are pockmarked from artillery fire. Finally, there is the vast American cemetery, a silent reminder of the human cost of war.

We boarded buses and moved inland, toward the town of St. Laurent-sur-Mer and then on to Colombières, where my father had told Lt. Roger Watson to go to the aid of the injured French children. I looked down a road that led east to Bricqueville. In that vicinity, I now knew, my father had treated Billy Melander of Tonawanda, New York. I stood in a church in Ste. Marguerite-d'Elle, the site of another aid station and likely where he had

Walter Carter placing flowers at the spot where his father was killed, Bois de Bretel, September 1997.

treated Capt. John Ryan and had shown him photographs of Tom and me. There, or perhaps in the Pagny family's chateau, my father had written his last letters to his wife and his parents.

A little farther southwest, at the west end of Road D-448, which runs alongside the Bois de Bretel, I stood with my family, the veterans, and our French hosts as Frank Wawrynovic addressed us. He recounted his experience—being shot while on a scouting mission, crawling back toward the American line, calling for help, being attended to by my father and the two medics, and watching in horror as they fell.

Near Frank stood a road sign covered with a banner. When he finished speaking, two of our French hosts drew back the banner and revealed the name: Captain Carter Road. This wonderful gesture was not a surprise—one of the French organizers of the trip had written to me about it. An honor guard presented the colors, a trumpeter played taps, and my children brought forward a bouquet of flowers, which I placed at the base of the sign. I spoke briefly, thanking the veterans and reading aloud from some of my father's letters, including the one to his friend John Morris. "It is rough as hell and I'll admit I fear for the future. However, I am happier here than anywhere else in the Army. A swell bunch of officers and men. One feels very close to these men and I want to do my best for them. I don't fear death per se, but it really depresses me to think that I may never see Fernie, Tom, and Walter Ford again."

Reboarding our buses, we drove along Captain Carter Road, stopping at an opening in a hedgerow. Here my father had gone to the aid of the wounded Frank. We followed Frank to the site, and he pointed out, across the narrow country road, the woods from which the German sniper had fired.

I tried to take it all in. I stared hard at the ground, vainly searching for blood stains. I turned toward the impenetrable woods across the road, wanting to plunge in to look for empty shell casings or other traces of the sniper. From his side of the road, I looked back to frame the picture he saw. I imagined American soldiers on the other side of the hedgerow, poised to attack or repel counterattack. I peered into the ploughed cornfield that was once an orchard, envisaging fallen combatants. It was too much. I knew I would have to come back, to

Walter Carter and his family—Bonnie, Catherine, and Norman—at Norval's grave, Colleville-sur-Mer, September 1997.

climb over the hedgerows, walk the field, search the woods, and feel the reverberations of my father's fear and determination.

The following day, at the American cemetery at Colleville-sur-Mer, a sergeant from the current Twenty-ninth Division escorted me and my family to my father's grave. We laid a bouquet at the base of the headstone and then embraced. I told my wife and children that I wished my father had known them—he would have loved and enjoyed them very much—but that I was glad that they knew him at last. A Frenchman approached and grasped our hands, tears streaming down his face.

We also attended a consecration ceremony at the Wall of Remembrance in St. Jean-de-Savigny. Dedicated to the men of the Twenty-ninth Division, the wall contained plaques bearing veterans' names, including my father's. There we met Pierre Labbé, a hard-working farmer and one of several Frenchmen who had built the wall with their own hands. Pierre bore the marks of his tough existence on the land—his skin was darkly tanned and he was missing several teeth and several fingers—and he made a profound impression on our children. When Pierre and Norman were engaged in small talk, Pierre suddenly exclaimed something in French and then walked away. Tears welled up in Norman's eyes. Turning to Bonnie, Catherine, and me, he translated Pierre's words: "Your grandfather died for us."

Our trip to Normandy was drawing to a close. I felt as if I had attended my father's funeral, fifty-three years after his death.

Back in Newton, I continued to reach out to other veterans and to my father's surviving classmates from the Medical College of Virginia. Many of my letters and phone calls led to nothing, but some yielded wonderful details of his life.

I wanted to share my father's story with anyone who would listen. In March 1998, at the invitation of a friend, I spoke at the Sunday morning service of the First Congregational Church in Weymouth, Massachusetts. It was an emotional challenge to speak in public about my father, my mother, my brother; about loss. In preparation I wrote and rewrote my remarks and then rehearsed them aloud. When the day came, the setting brought back memories of attending church with my mother and murmuring "Our Father" while thinking of my own. I got through my speech, and the congregation received me warmly.

Over the next four years I gave a dozen similar talks. I was invariably received with kind attention, validating my belief that the story of Norval and Fernie Carter was important. I remained in touch with Frank and Stella Wawrynovic, whose friendship has meant so much to me. When historians write that those who lived through the Great Depression and World War II were this nation's "greatest generation," they are speaking of people like Frank and Stella. They are also speaking about my parents.

After our pilgrimage to Normandy I did not hear from Frank for several months. Eventually I received a long, reflective, apologetic letter from him. He had been busy, he explained, but there was something more. Like so many other veterans, he had spent nearly a lifetime trying to put the war and its violence and horror behind him, to get on with the ordinary rituals of life that seem so extraordinary in the midst of death, misery, and terror. "While the war never fully leaves our minds," Frank wrote, "any interruption that again gives the war priority over the normal daily routine . . . can be very painful." After returning home from the trip, it took Frank several months to regain that "normal daily routine."

Above all, the visit to Normandy reminded him that his generation is passing. Those who experienced the carnage on the beaches of Normandy or the trial of rearing children by themselves while trying to suppress anxiety and fear will soon be silent. Others will remember, though, and tell the stories handed down to them. Frank wrote:

"We must realize that time is running out for those of us who survived the D-Day landing and the battle of the hedgerows. Too much of historical significance has already been lost. Too many of our comrades have already passed on, leaving untold the stories of their heroism. . . . Writers can try to reconstruct events as they had occurred, but unless they had actually been there, they can only report on, but not express, the heroism of individual actions, the . . . emotions of those about whom they write."

For more than half a century, my father's story remained lost—to us, his loved ones, as well as to history. My mother's grief, as well as the joy of her life before the war, would have remained unexpressed had those letters not been found. I would not have met Frank and Stella and so many other veterans and friends of my father's had I not embarked on a journey whose end I could not have imagined.

In a letter to his friend John Morris on May 15, 1944, as he was preparing for D-Day, my father tried to explain why he had volunteered for combat, but words failed him. "It is impossible to know why," he confided, "my feelings are all mixed up about it." I do not know why, either, but I no longer believe it is important to know.

Perhaps my father, realizing he might not come home, was determined to make himself known to his children through these letters. My mother joined in his purpose by saving them for us. She knew we would find them.

I am left with a legacy of words—the words of two people who were very much in love, who spent childhood days together when the twentieth century was young, who drove off in a car one day to get married, who expected to spend their lives together, and who gave life to me. They were still young when events far from West Virginia changed their lives and their dreams. Indeed, the war changed everything—everything, that is, except their love. Their stories, like their love, will never die.

Many of the men who rest near my father on the windswept bluffs of northern France left behind children who have no memories. They were too young to remember the hugs they received and returned, the smiles, the laughter, the funny faces, the tears. Some were born after their fathers left home one day in a soldier's uniform, never to return. They have no trove of letters and testimonials. They are still among us, the children of World War II. They are closer to the end of their lives than to the beginning. But just as the war never truly ends for the combat veteran, it also has not ended for the fatherless. They are the war's hidden casualties, their wounds invisible. Perhaps they take comfort in the knowledge that today's world, though still frightening and violent, is better off because of those GIs who lie in cemeteries in Normandy and throughout the world. In peaceful, green places, they bear mute witness not to the power of modern weaponry but to the mysterious power of human courage and sacrifice.

When my parents were children, men who fought in the Civil War still walked the streets and lanes of America's cities and towns. They were men from another time, men who spoke of places children knew only from history books—Gettysburg, Sharpsburg, Antietam. They were vanishing, and before long they were gone, their stories with them.

In a few years the veterans of World War II will seem as ghostlike to the children of the twenty-first century as Civil War veterans did to children of my parents' generation. Place names that once conjured up images of heroism and death—Iwo Jima, Salerno, Omaha Beach—now are heard only in the classroom, if there. Few, if any, tributes are directed to the remarkable women who held families together while their husbands, fathers, sons, and brothers went off to war. The world moves on, as it must.

Still, as long as there are graves above Omaha Beach, we dare not forget the men and women who fought and sacrificed not for themselves but for us. Men and women like the people I met on my own journey of discovery—Dad and Mom.

Acknowledgments

My discovery of my father would not have been possible without his letters, and I am grateful to my mother for saving them. Dr. John Morris—my father's boyhood friend, schoolmate, colleague, and to a large extent my surrogate father—contributed much to my original image of Dad as a lovable hero. Several organizations and their members opened their hearts and many doors for me: the American World War II Orphans Network, Normandy Allies, the Joan Edwards School of Medicine at Marshall University, and especially the Twenty-ninth Division Association. Frank Wawrynovic poured his heart out in conveying the circumstances of my father's death and helped memorialize my father's name. Joe Balkoski, author of two outstanding books on the Normandy campaign, shared his unmatched knowledge of and reverence for what America and its Allies accomplished there, at times as we walked together along the Twenty-ninth Division's path from Omaha Beach to St.-Lô. Tom Gorman, Martha Holden, Beth Bullard, and Daphne Abeel read drafts along the way and helped me shape them for the general reader. My agent, John Wright, recognized the merit of the story; enlisted the artist and craftsman, Terry Golway, who could make it come alive; and persisted until he found the astute editors at Smithsonian Books. My children's desire to know their grandfather, and through his story to know me, was a primary motivation, and my wife's supportive love and patient understanding, as well as her delight in trips to France, made it all possible. Thank you, Bonnie, Norman, Catherine, and all the rest. I am, of course, responsible for any and all errors that may remain.